MISSION AND MONEY:

A CHS 2000 REPORT ON FINANCE, ADVANCEMENT, AND GOVERNANCE

SISTER MARY E. TRACY, SNJM

NATIONAL CATHOLIC EDUCATIONAL ASSOCIATION

Published in the United States of America by the National Catholic Educational Association

ISBN 1-55833-260-X

TABLE OF CONTENTS

LIST OF EXHIBITS

TRENDS AND HIGHLIGHTS IN CATHOLIC HIGH SCHOOLS

- 90% of all Catholic high schools report having development offices. The majority of development offices were initiated in the mid-eighties.

- The average tuition for the 9th grade in 1998-1999 was $4,289, a 5.4% increase over the previous year's tuition.

- The average annual salary for a beginning lay teacher with no previous teaching experience with a B.A./B.S. (excluding benefits) in fall 1998 was $21,300. The average top salary for an experienced teacher with an M.A./M.S. (excluding benefits) was $42,300.

- The average annual salary for school heads in 1998-1999 was $60,900.

- Compensation for priests and religious continues to move closer to lay equivalence. The average compensation package in 1998 for religious women was $28,800, up from $22,000 in 1992 and $24,600 in 1994.

- Priests and religious represent, on average, 6% of faculties in Catholic high schools, down from 10% in 1994.

- Financial aid was awarded, on average, to 22% of Catholic high school students in 1998. The primary criterion for awarding aid was evidence of financial need.

- The total amount of financial aid offered by the average Catholic high school in 1997-1998 (including scholarships, tuition reductions, grants, work-study and support from sponsoring parishes, dioceses, and religious orders) was $246,000.

- 46% of the heads of Catholic high schools in 1999 held a title other than principal.

- More than one third of Catholic high schools in 1999 were running capital campaigns.

- 95% of all Catholic high schools used a salary scale in 1999 to determine faculty compensation.

- 80% of Catholic high schools reported having a governing board in 1999. 100% of private independent Catholic schools and 62% of arch/diocesan schools reported having a governing board in 1999.

ACKNOWLEDGEMENTS

I am grateful to the participating schools' leaders for investing substantial time and research in responding to the questions.

Four heads of Catholic high schools participated in our pilot questionnaire: Mary Ellen Barnes (principal of Archbishop Williams High School, Braintree, MA), Catherine Karl, Ph.D. (president of Queen of Peace High School, Chicago, IL), James Pecchenino (president of Central Catholic High School, Modesto, CA), and Elizabeth Swift (principal of Holy Names Academy, Seattle, WA). I thank each reviewer for critical suggestions that enhanced the final questionnaire.

The Executive Committee of the Secondary Schools Department and the *CHS 2000* Advisory Committee inspired *Mission and Money* with forward momentum consistent with the impetus underlying *CHS 2000*.

The staff of the NCEA Secondary Schools Department is to be commended for realizing the importance of this report to our constituents. Michael Guerra, *CHS 2000* project director, has enlightened this focused account by providing direction, wisdom, and a discerning intellect. Eileen Emerson was masterful in organizing the questionnaire's distribution and bringing order out of the chaos of hundreds of completed documents, each with 155 different sets of numbers and terms. Linda McCullogh's technical expertise was invaluable in the presentation of data, which formed the foundation for its extensive interpretation. Brian Vaccaro, with steady head and hand, extended his well-developed editing skills and technological wizardry to the manuscript. Clearly, *Mission and Money: A CHS 2000 Report on Finance, Advancement, and Governance* reflects the efforts of a conscientious and committed Secondary Schools departmental team.

Béagán agus a rá go maith.

Sr. Mary E. Tracy, SNJM
Washington, DC
St. Patrick's Day, 2001

INTRODUCTION

M*ission and Money: A CHS 2000 Report on Finance, Advancement, and Governance* is your tool. All are encouraged to make the best possible use of this resource. The national trends and regional variances could serve as useful benchmarks for institutional planning. The data collected and interpreted for this report indicate a world of promise for Catholic high schools and the generations served by these schools. The prospect of a bright future is supported by the trends, highlights, and figures presented here.

The figures resulting from this study serve largely as signs of institutional vitality: full schools, mature annual funds, successful capital campaigns, growing endowments, and operational governance structures. While celebrating the sustained progression of Catholic secondary schools, schools that seem to falter or backtrack fiscally should not be overlooked; as the majority of schools flourish, a small percentage shows financial strain. Even while new Catholic high schools are being established successfully, there are still those few, some with long histories, who, sadly, could be forced to close their doors.

Like an X-ray, these data presented in *Mission and Money* show contrasts and trends and serve as partial images of the fiscal health status of Catholic high schools. A full examination of the data requires the appropriate faith perspective to flesh out meaningful levels of institutional wellness. The statistics alone cannot truly express the complete fiscal story of Catholic high schools. Spirituality embodies the institutional flesh and blood that bring the bare-bones data to life.

As *Mission and Money* asserts, in the Catholic high school, money enlivens the implementation of mission, and mission gives meaning to money. The impact of the gift of Catholic secondary education rises exponentially as millions of graduates of Catholic high schools take on the world and carry this gift as their mission into ever expanding spheres of influence.

Exhibit 0.1 profiles the distribution of the national sample used in the initial questionnaire. The data from that national survey were used to produce *CHS 2000: A First Look* (Guerra, 1998).

Exhibit 0.1
Representative Distribution of the Responding Schools
(by Governance and Region)

	Mission and Money CHS 2000		
Governance	**N**	**%**	**% of schools (1997)**
Diocesan	65	32%	33%
Parochial	25	12%	12%
Interparochial	22	11%	11%
Private: religious community sponsored	73	36%	33%
Private: independent	20	10%	11%

	Mission and Money CHS 2000		
Region	**N**	**%**	**% of schools (1997)**
New England (CT, ME, MA, NH, RI, VT)	15	7%	8%
Mideast (DE, DC, MD, NJ, NY, PA)	56	28%	27%
Great Lakes (IL, IN, MI, OH, WI)	39	20%	21%
Plains (IA, KS, MN, MO, NE, ND, SD)	24	12%	12%
Southeast (AL, AR, FL, GA, KY, LA, MS, NC, SC, TN, VA, WV)	32	16%	14%
West/Far West (AK, AZ, CA, CO, HI, ID, MT, NV, NM, OK, OR, TX, UT, WA, WY)	35	17%	18%

CHAPTER 1

ACCESS AND DIVERSITY

FINANCIAL AID: HALLMARK OF THE CATHOLIC MISSION

Most Catholic high schools indicate a notable commitment to providing financial aid to students. When asked to describe the extent of their financial aid programs, the majority of schools indicated that many, most, or all students who needed financial assistance received aid. This level of commitment to low and moderate-income families is consistent with the NCEA Secondary Schools Department's reports in 1992 and 1994 and surely stretches back to the earliest beginnings of Catholic schools.

Exhibit 1.1 shows that 73% of Catholic high schools award financial aid to "most" or "all" who express need. Only 5% of schools indicate that aid is limited to a relatively small percentage who request it.

Private and interparochial schools indicate aid allocation to greater percentages of students than arch/diocesan and parochial schools; the financial aid distribution follows proportionately the tuition levels in the schools: private and independent schools' rates are higher than those in diocesan and parochial schools.

Exhibit 1.1
Financial Aid Recipient Profile of Catholic High Schools
(National Average of all Catholic High Schools)

28%	All students who need aid receive some aid
45%	Most (75-90%) students who express need receive aid
16%	Many (50-74%) students who need aid receive it
6%	Some (25-49%) receive it
5%	Financial aid is available for a small percentage (1-24%) of those who request it

---

Governance

	Diocesan	Parochial	Inter-parochial	Private: religious community-sponsored	Private: independent
All students who need aid receive some aid	21%	17.4%	47.6%	32.9%	26.3%
Most (75-90%) students who express need receive aid	46.8%	21.7%	42.9%	45.7%	68.4%
Many (50-74%) students who need aid receive it	22.6%	34.8%	0	11.4%	5.3%
Some (25-49%) receive it	4.8%	8.7%	4.8%	8.6%	/
Financial aid is available for a small percentage (1-24%) of those who request it	4.8%	17.4%	4.8%	1.4%	/

Region

	New England	Mideast	Great Lakes	Plains	Southeast	West/Far West
All students who need aid receive some aid	30.8%	14.8%	31.6%	47.8%	24.1%	33.3%
Most (75-90%) students who express need receive aid	38.5%	50%	36.8%	43.5%	55.2%	48.5%
Many (50-74%) students who need aid receive it	30.8%	18.5%	18.4%	4.3%	13.8%	12.1%
Some (25-49%) receive it	/	11.1%	7.9%	4.3%	/	6.1%
Financial aid is available for a small percentage (1-24%) of those who request it	/	5.6%	5.3%	/	6.9%	/

The dollar value of the average grant, $1,467, represents 36% of the mean tuition of the ninth grade in 1998-1999, up from 34% reported in the department's most recent statistical study of 1994, *Dollars and Sense: Catholic High Schools and Their Finances* (M. Guerra). The average grant of $1,467 reflects growth over the 1994 average grant of $1,098 and that amount had risen from the 1992 grant of $996. In general, financial aid has been increased annually at rates at least equal to those schools' tuition increases, generally exceeding inflation.

About 22% of the typical school's applicants receive financial aid, down slightly from 24% in 1994, and that figure was an increase over the 1992 reported level of 19%. While financial aid generally has kept pace with tuition, the growth of financial aid is obvious during the past decade, a trend that makes the case for Catholic schools' continuing commitment to the underserved and working class communities in our cities and regions throughout the country.

Catholic high schools are awarding financial aid in greater amounts. The total amount of financial aid as a line item in the operating budget is impressive. The 1997-1998 data reveal a clear institutional priority and, in some cases, extraordinary effort. The median amount of $140,100 has risen from the 1994 level of $96,400 and the 1992 amount of $69,000. The total financial aid funding has more than doubled in seven years. The aggregate amounts are greater among the private schools, i.e. those sponsored by religious communities and those governed as independent schools; the parochial and interparochial schools, mostly smaller in size and charging lower tuition rates, generally offer more modest levels of total financial aid funding.

The total amount of financial aid, (including scholarships, tuition reductions, grants, work-study, and support from sponsoring parishes, dioceses, and religious orders) awarded in 1997-1998 by Catholic high schools is profiled in Exhibit 1.1.

The terms "mean" and "median" are used throughout this book. Median refers to the halfway point in a list of items, a point where half of the items would be above the point and half below the point. Mean refers to the average, the sum of a set of items divided by the number of items (e.g. the mean of 2, 3, and 19 is 8; the median of 2, 3, and 19 is 3).

Exhibit 1.2
Total Financial Aid Distribution Profile of the Catholic High School

	Mean	Median
National	$245,950	$139,142
Governance		
Diocesan	$224,591	$155,000
Parochial	$80,433	$39,000
Interparochial	$64,915	$41,408
Private: religious community-sponsored	$300,336	$180,000
Private: independent	$474,693	$338,262
Region		
New England	$405,671	$196,465
Mideast	$295,801	$150,000
Great Lakes	$279,871	$196,000
Plains	$232,076	$90,000
Southeast	$121,269	$83,000
West/Far West	$189,676	$148,500

The primary criterion for awarding aid is economic need (98%) as it was in 1994 (98%). About half of the Catholic high schools consider a student's academic record in finalizing aid allocation; roughly one in five schools takes race or ethnic origin into consideration in determining aid; less than 1% of Catholic high schools report that they base financial aid on athletic promise. Most but not all (71%) schools offer partial or full tuition discounts to children of faculty and/or staff. All of these criteria are consistent with trends reported five years ago. Catholic high schools continue to demonstrate inclusivity and non-discriminatory practices in financial aid determination.

When asked to indicate which criteria are considered, in part or in whole, in allocating financial aid, academic record or promise was reported as important by slightly over half of the schools, yet just under half reported that academic progress was not a consideration.

Exhibit 1.3 shows the percentage of schools using various criteria to award financial aid in 1998.

Exhibit 1.3
Criteria Used in Awarding Financial Aid

Yes	No	
52%	47%	Academic record or promise
8%	92%	Athletic record or promise
98%	2%	Financial need
18%	82%	Racial or ethnic origin
3%	96%	Vocational intention
72%	28%	Faculty/Staff children

When asked to indicate the one criterion that receives the greatest importance in awarding financial aid, 98% reported financial need, 2% indicated academic promise, and only one school considered race or ethnic origin as the most important factor. No school gave the greatest weight to a student's athletic record or promise, nor did any school see vocational intention as the most important criterion.

As tuition and fee rates increase steadily, financial aid becomes increasingly important to Catholic high schools. In 1998-1999, Catholic high schools awarded $257 million to 175,000 students, an impressive profile that represents a substantial commitment to low and moderate-income families. These figures compare favorably with the 1993-1994 research, which reported a collective financial commitment of $150 million to 140,000 students.

Exhibit 1.4 shows the dollar value of the average financial aid allocation for one student in the Catholic high school.

Exhibit 1.4
National Average: Financial Aid Allocation for One Student
(by Governance and Region)

	Mean	Median
National	$1467	$1000
Governance		
Diocesan	$1008	$850
Parochial	$1036	$917
Interparochial	$788	$800
Private: religious community-sponsored	$1694	$1500
Private: independent	$3307	$2000
Region		
New England	$3008	$1366
Mideast	$1428	$1000
Great Lakes	$1229	$1000
Plains	$1230	$955
Southeast	$1132	$1000
West/Far West	$1716	$1450

Exhibit 1.5
National Percentages of Students Applying for Financial Aid
(by Governance and Region)

	Mean	Median
National	27%	21%
Governance		
Diocesan	29%	20%
Parochial	27%	15%
Interparochial	16%	16%
Private: religious community-sponsored	27%	25%
Private: independent	30%	27%
Region		
New England	42%	30%
Mideast	29%	25%
Great Lakes	29%	24%
Plains	24%	21%
Southeast	17%	18%
West/Far West	27%	21%

FINANCIAL AID AND FAMILY INCOME FOR THE CATHOLIC HIGH SCHOOL

Perception of family income is important in understanding the economic diversity represented in Catholic high schools. As reported by the head of school, the data indicate that Catholic secondary schools are serving increased numbers of relatively poor students compared to five years ago. 12% of families served are believed to be in the low–income category (less than $20,000) compared to the 1994 report of 7%. 66% of families in Catholic high schools are seen as modest or middle-income households. 15% of the families served by Catholic high schools are perceived by the head of school as being upper-income households ($81,000 - $120,000) and 7% as high income (greater than $120,000).

Measured by the increased percentage of low-income families served, the expanded numbers of students benefiting from financial aid, and the enhanced dollar value of the average financial aid grant, Catholic high schools are widening their tents. While some have suggested a creeping elitism in Catholic schools, these data indicate that Catholic high schools are far from elite. These schools, as a group, are maintaining their commitment to socioeconomic diversity.

The following five tables show the economic diversity represented in Catholic high schools. Heads of school were asked to give their best estimates of what percent of students in their schools come from families with each of the following gross annual incomes.

Exhibit 1.6
National Economic Diversity Represented in Catholic High Schools
(by Governance and Region)

Low income (under $20,000)
Modest income ($21,000-$40,000)
Middle income ($41,000-$80,000)
Upper-middle income ($81,000-$120,000)
Upper income (Over $121,000)

Low income (under $20,000)	Mean	Median
National	12%	5%
Governance		
Diocesan	11.5%	5%
Parochial	15.8%	10%
Interparochial	8.7%	9.5%
Private: religious community-sponsored	12.2%	5%
Private: independent	10.2%	6.5%
Region		
New England	12.1%	12%
Mideast	12.4%	5%
Great Lakes	13.6%	5%
Plains	9.5%	7%
Southeast	7.7%	5%
West/Far West	11.3%	5%

Modest Income ($21,000-$40,000)	Mean	Median
National	30%	25%
Governance		
Diocesan	29.6%	25%
Parochial	43.6%	42.5%
Interparochial	37.6%	32.5%
Private: religious community-sponsored	25.1%	20%
Private: independent	24.6%	20.5%
Region		
New England	30.3%	20%
Mideast	31.1%	26%
Great Lakes	30.5%	27.5%
Plains	36%	30%
Southeast	29.2%	22.5%
West/Far West	24.8%	20%

Middle Income ($41,000-$80,000)	Mean	Median
National	36%	36%
Governance		
Diocesan	38.7%	40%
Parochial	30.8%	29%
Interparochial	38.1%	40%
Private: religious community-sponsored	36.5%	37%
Private: independent	28.5%	25%
Region		
New England	33.3%	32.5%
Mideast	37%	37%
Great Lakes	38.6%	40%
Plains	34.1%	30%
Southeast	36.9%	35.5%
West/Far West	34.9%	33.5%

Upper-middle Income ($81,0000-$120,000)	Mean	Median
National	15%	10%
Governance		
Diocesan	14.5%	10%
Parochial	7%	5%
Interparochial	11.1%	6.5%
Private: religious community-sponsored	17.1%	15%
Private: independent	22.9%	15%
Region		
New England	16.2%	11.5%
Mideast	13.4%	10%
Great Lakes	11.9%	10%
Plains	13.2%	10%
Southeast	19%	18%
West/Far West	19.1%	20%

Upper Income (Over $121,000)	Mean	Median
National	7%	5%
Governance		
Diocesan	5.5%	3%
Parochial	2.8%	0%
Interparochial	5.1%	5%
Private: religious community-sponsored	9.0%	5%
Private: independent	13.7%	10%
Region		
New England	7.8%	3.5%
Mideast	6.1%	2%
Great Lakes	5.9%	5%
Plains	7%	1%
Southeast	7%	5%
West/Far West	10%	10%

Chapter 2

Sources of Income

Tuition covers roughly 80% of the average Catholic high school's operating budget. This figure has increased from 75% in 1994. The percentage is considerably less in parochial and diocesan schools and somewhat higher in religious community-sponsored and private, independent schools. Subsidies (religious community, parish, or diocesan) represent about 4% of the typical operating budget for the Catholic high school, down from 6% in 1994. Parish and diocesan subsidies benefit parish and diocesan schools for the most part and religious community subsidies are present in private schools. In all cases, subsidies have been declining for the past decade as a source of income.

Contributed services are down to 2% from 3% in 1994, but the percentage of the operating budget is so low that the reduction is meaningless – except to affirm that contributed services are steadily being phased out as a reliable budgetary line item. When asked if women religious were paid on the same salary schedule as lay teachers, 43% of the schools said yes; 40% indicated that men religious were paid lay equivalent salaries; and 28% affirmed the salary schedule for diocesan priests. In response to the same question, 41% indicated that no women religious were on staff.

From a national perspective, contributed services have become a relatively insignificant line item in the typical operating budget, the result of both declining numbers of religious on staff and institutional efforts toward putting all professionals, lay and religious, on the same salary scales. Few schools report exceptional situations where relatively large numbers of religious serve and where their contributed services still provide substantial annual operating income. Other anecdotal reports reveal praiseworthy efforts of religious communities who are investing substantial annual and capital financial contributions in their sponsored schools although members of the sponsoring religious community are no longer actively serving as teachers or administrators at the school.

Exhibit 2.1 represents a sample operating revenue budget for the average Catholic high school. Each line item would not necessarily be found in every school, even within the same school governance type. All amounts are averages and represent a fiscal picture painted with the broadest statistical brush.

Exhibit 2.1
Sample Operating Revenue for the Average Catholic High School (1997-1998)

Tuition and fees	$2,619,000
Contributed services	$65,000
Religious community grant/subsidy	$16,000
Parish grant/subsidy	$75,000
Diocesan grant/subsidy	$48,000
Annual fund-alumni/ae	$76,000
Annual fund-parents	$39,000
Special events	$111,000
Auxiliary services	$52,000
Federal government funding	$12,000
State government funding	$19,000
Endowment income transferred to operating budget	$59,000
All other income	$175,000
Total operating budget	$3,366,000

OPERATING INCOME BY GOVERNANCE

Private schools generally report higher operating budgets than arch/diocesan or parochial schools. Consistent with trend data reported in 1994, subsidies are considerably lower in private schools, and play a smaller role in the budgets of these schools. The variances in budget size can be attributed to enrollment differences and tuition levels. Generally, tuition in private schools is higher than those in arch/diocesan or parochial schools. (See Exhibit 2.5.)

Exhibit 2.2 shows national mean and median annual operating budgets for 1999 according to governance type and region.

Exhibit 2.2
National Mean and Median Annual Operating Budgets for 1999
(by Governance and Region)

	Mean	Median
National	$3,366,000	$2,770,500
Governance		
Diocesan	$3,242,750	$2,806,000
Parochial	$1,725,900	$1,242,000
Interparochial	$1,461,667	$1,200,000
Private: religious community-sponsored	$4,018,855	$3,793,000
Private: independent	$4,165,667	$4,291,500
Region		
New England	$3,069,857	$2,758,000
Mideast	$3,205,673	$2,801,500
Great Lakes	$3,369,714	$3,118,000
Plains	$2,997,619	$2,080,000
Southeast	$3,136,857	$2,406,500
West/Far West	$3,602,333	$3,104,000

TUITION RATES AND PER PUPIL COSTS

Tuition in private schools is generally higher than in arch/diocesan or parochial schools, consistent with the 1994 data. In analyzing all schools across all governance and regional variations, the average 9th grade tuition in 1998-1999 was $4,289, compared to the 1994 figure of $3,316, a 29% increase over five years. This increase reflects, generally, the tendency to increase tuition costs at rates slightly greater than inflation.

Exhibit 2.3 shows the relative increases in tuition of average Catholic high schools from 1997 to 1998 and the variances among grade levels in costs and in percentages of tuition increases.

Exhibit 2.3
Tuition Increase from 1997-1998

	1998-1999 tuition	1997-1998 tuition
Grade 9	$4,289 (5.7% increase)	$4,055
Grade 10	$4,297 (6% increase)	$4,053
Grade 11	$4,433 (9.3% increase)	$4,054
Grade 12	$4,304 (6.6% increase)	$4,038

Per pupil costs for the average Catholic high school in 1998-1999 were $5,571, a significant (35%) increase over the 1994 report of $4,120.

Exhibit 2.4 profiles the levels of funding provided by tuition in the typical Catholic high school. There are significant variations among governance types and regions. On average, tuition represents 78% of the operating revenue, up from 75% in 1994 and 73% in 1992. While Exhibit 2.4 shows that tuition revenues are much higher in private schools, the operating budgets are also higher, so the 78% is applicable across all schools surveyed.

Exhibit 2.4
Income from Tuition and Fees

	Mean	Median
National	$2,619,088	$2,068,000
Governance		
Diocesan	$2,529,705	$2,200,000
Parochial	$1,005,714	$1,049,000
Interparochial	$990,182	$639,000
Private: religious community-sponsored	$3,474,127	$2,784,000
Private: independent	$3,422,500	$3,182,500
Region		
New England	$2,407,143	$1,979,000
Mideast	$3,336,964	$2,321,000
Great Lakes	$2,118,222	$1,732,000
Plains	$1,909,391	$1,200,000
Southeast	$2,266,556	$2,000,000
West/Far West	$2,853,848	$2,739,000

Exhibit 2.3 shows increases in tuition rates from 1997 to 1998, exclusive of additional fees, for a student who is the only one from a given family enrolled in the same school.

Exhibit 2.5 represents mean and median tuition for 1998-1999 according to governance type and region.

Exhibit 2.5
Mean and Median Tuition for 1998-1999
(by Governance and Region)

Grade 9: 1998-1999	Mean	Median
National	$4,289	$4,000
Governance		
Diocesan	$3,815	$3,700
Parochial	$2,780	$2,775
Interparochial	$2,296	$2,400
Private: religious community-sponsored	$5,002	$4,700
Private: independent	$7,362	$5,312
Region		
New England	$7,076	$4,785
Mideast	$4,500	$4,370
Great Lakes	$3,631	$3,653
Plains	$3,367	$3,785
Southeast	$3,525	$3,280
West/Far West	$4,956	$4,720

Grade 10: 1998-1999	Mean	Median
National	$4,297	$4,000
Governance		
Diocesan	$3,812	$3,650
Parochial	$2,782	$2,775
Interparochial	$2,308	$2,425
Private: religious community-sponsored	$4,993	$4,700
Private: independent	$7,373	$5,313
Region		
New England	$7,031	$4,785
Mideast	$4,500	$4,370
Great Lakes	$3,631	$3,653
Plains	$3,374	$3,485
Southeast	$3,575	$3,300
West/Far West	$4,956	$4,720

Grade 11: 1998-1999	Mean	Median
National	$4,433	$4,000
Governance		
Diocesan	$3,813	$3,650
Parochial	$2,782	$2,775
Interparochial	$2,312	$2,425
Private: religious community-sponsored	$5,002	$4,700
Private: independent	$7,373	$5,600
Region		
New England	$7,076	$4,785
Mideast	$4,500	$4,370
Great Lakes	$3,631	$3,790
Plains	$3,381	$3,485
Southeast	$3,575	$3,300
West/Far West	$4,956	$4,720
Grade 12: 1998-1999	**Mean**	**Median**
National	$4,304	$4,000
Governance		
Diocesan	$3,806	$3,625
Parochial	$2,782	$2,775
Interparochial	$2,313	$2,425
Private: religious community-sponsored	$5,006	$4,700
Private: independent	$7,373	$5,312
Region		
New England	$7,076	$4,785
Mideast	$4,505	$4,370
Great Lakes	$3,631	$3,653
Plains	$3,393	$3,625
Southeast	$3,542	$3,280
West/Far West	$4,956	$4,720

Tuition levels are consistently highest in private independent schools and lowest in parochial and interparochial schools. Tuition rates for private religious community-sponsored schools are slightly less than they are for the independent schools.

Rates in New England are notably higher than in other geographic regions; this probably reflects the relatively high number of private schools in the northeast. Tuition rates in the West are relatively higher than those in the middle of the country, where a number of parochial and interparochial schools are located, and in the southeast.

Chapter 3

How is Money Spent
in the Catholic High School?

Exhibit 3.1 shows the average operating expenses for a Catholic high school in 1997-1998. Faculty and staff salaries and benefits account for 69% of all operating costs, up from 64% in 1994. 11% of the operating budget is directed to benefits, down slightly from 12% in 1994.

Contributed services, down from 3% to 2% of the budget, account for $61,000 in 1997-1998 in contrast to the 1994 figure of $57,000.

Maintenance costs account for 7% of the average school's operating budget.

Exhibit 3.1
Operating Expenses for the Catholic High School (1997-1998)

Salaries (lay professional staff including development office)	$1,346,000
Salaries (religious professional faculty/staff-actual cash)	$158,000
Contributed services	$61,000
Other salaries (general office maintenance but not auxiliary)	$237,000
Benefits (FICA, health, retirement, etc.)	$322,000
Net costs of auxiliary services	$65,000
Maintenance	$208,000
All other operating costs	$606,000
Total operating costs	$3,003,000

Compensation: Head of School

The typical lay head of school's salary in 1998-1999 was $60,900. Five years earlier, this figure was $51,000. The survey revealed the minimum salary for the head of one of the sampled schools was $26,129 and the maximum was $137,500. For those schools with a president or head of school with a title other than principal, the average principal's salary was $51,600, and the maximum was $86,000.

According to the National Association of Secondary School Principals (NASSP), the national public school mean salary for a high school principal for the same year was in the range of $76,914 (low) to $82,162 (high). The National Association of Independent Schools (NAIS) reports the mean salary for the head of a secondary school for 1999 was $120,365, with variations depending on school size and enrollment. The Catholic secondary school's salary for the head of school is about 79% of the NASSP reported average salary, and 50% of the NAIS figure.

COMPENSATION: WOMEN RELIGIOUS

Among the schools in the sample, 80% report that they have some religious women on staff. Of these, 43% are paid salaries according to the same schedules and criteria as lay faculty members; 57% are not paid lay equivalent salaries. The percentage of 43% is up from 27% in 1994 and that figure was an increase over 22% in 1992. These data suggest a clear trend toward lay equivalence in compensation of women religious.

A small majority of those schools operating with a stipend structure for women religious provide the same salary for all women religious on staff, regardless of education, experience, or responsibility. The compensation level (total of salary, benefits, housing, transportation, and stipends) of $28,767 is up from $24,600 reported five years ago by the Secondary Schools Department.

Exhibit 3.2 shows the average compensation (total of salary, benefits, housing, transportation, and stipends) for women religious who teach full-time in Catholic high schools.

Exhibit 3.2
National Average: Compensation for Women Religious Who Teach Full-time

	Mean	Median
National	$28,767	$27,090
Governance		
Diocesan	$27,531	$26,000
Parochial	$27,320	$26,145
Interparochial	$24,599	$25,220
Private: religious community-sponsored	$30,779	$29,482
Private: independent	$35,133	$31,650
Region		
New England	$25,518	$24,722
Mideast	$26,566	$26,180
Great Lakes	$30,053	$27,500
Plains	$27,146	$28,500
Southeast	$28,241	$26,000
West/Far West	$35,355	$33,600

COMPENSATION: BROTHERS AND PRIESTS

Compensation differs among brothers, diocesan priests, and religious priests. The average annual compensation (total of salary, benefits, housing, transportation, and stipends) for a diocesan priest who teaches full-time in a Catholic high school is $23,252; the average salary for religious (order) priests and brothers is $31,764. The average compensation for diocesan priests ($23,252) is up from $18,500 five years ago, and the stipend ($31,764) for religious (order) priests and brothers reflects an increase from $21,100 in 1994. When asked if all men religious received the same compensation regardless of education or experience, roughly half of those schools to which the question applied indicated that there was some variation.

Exhibit 3.3 shows the compensation figures for brothers and priests according to governance type and region of school.

Exhibit 3.3
National Compensation Figures for Brothers and Priests
(by Governance and Region)

	Mean	Median
National	$31,764	$31,378
Governance		
Diocesan	$28,928	$28,700
Parochial	$27,747	$27,747
Interparochial	$25,000	$25,000
Private: religious community-sponsored	$33,476	$32,664
Private: independent	$38,083	$31,885
Region		
New England	$30,200	$31,000
Mideast	$33,728	$31,491
Great Lakes	$29,447	$31,711
Plains	$29,176	$27,000
Southeast	$27,715	$30,000
West/Far West	$38,913	$36,810

COMPENSATION: LAY TEACHERS

In every case, Catholic high schools have made some progress in the areas of salaries and benefits. The average salary paid to a beginning lay teacher with a B.A./B.S. and no experience has increased from $19,000 in 1994 to $21,300 in 1999, representing just a 12% increase.

The median salary (excluding benefits) paid to full-time lay teachers has risen to $30,242 from $23,100 in 1994. Exhibit 3.4 shows some variance across regional and governance type.

Exhibit 3.4
National Median Salary (Excluding Benefits) Paid to Full-time Lay Teachers
(by Governance and Region)

	Mean	Median
National	$30,242	$29,800
Governance		
Diocesan	$31,045	$30,344
Parochial	$24,451	$25,220
Interparochial	$24,929	$24,459
Private: religious community-sponsored	$32,919	$32,000
Private: independent	$30,005	$30,214
Region		
New England	$31,638	$34,000
Mideast	$32,769	$32,000
Great Lakes	$29,569	$28,317
Plains	$28,221	$27,500
Southeast	$27,563	$26,812
West/Far West	$31,700	$31,321

Exhibits 3.4, 3.5 and 3.6 show that average compensation levels are relatively modest in contrast to any number of public school scales. The data suggest that schools are exploring the relationship between tuition and compensation, and, as the next part of the report will show, advancement is playing an increasingly important part in the financial mix. While tuition represents about 80% of the average Catholic high school revenue, compensation (salaries and benefits) accounts for about 69% of the typical Catholic high school's annual expenses. The NAIS data reveal $36,167 as the median salary paid in 1999 to a full-time teacher in an independent school.

Exhibit 3.5 shows the highest **scheduled** salary for an experienced lay teacher with an M.A./M.S. (excluding benefits). The maximum salary reported for an experienced lay teacher was $62,000.

Exhibit 3.5
Highest Scheduled Salary for an Experienced Lay Teacher
(by Governance and Region)

	Mean	Median
National	$39,107	$39,235
Governance		
Diocesan	$40,588	$41,407
Parochial	$33,418	$33,719
Interparochial	$31,132	$34,275
Private: religious community-sponsored	$41,950	$41,290
Private: independent	$36,883	$41,000
Region		
New England	$36,566	$41,309
Mideast	$43,584	$41,407
Great Lakes	$37,453	$37,783
Plains	$38,042	$39,836
Southeast	$34,669	$33,680
West/Far West	$40,318	$41,767

The table shows that the mean is $36,883 for private independent schools, yet the mean salary for private religious community-sponsored schools is $41,950. The median for private independent schools is $41,000. These figures suggest that either private independent schools employ larger than average numbers of faculty at the beginning levels of salary scales or that other schools have greater numbers of veteran teachers.

Exhibit 3.6 shows the highest salary of the average Catholic high school **actually paid** to a lay teacher in 1998-1999.

Exhibit 3.6
Highest Salary Actually Paid to a Lay Teacher
(by Governance and Region)

	Mean	Median
National	$42,295	$41,809
Governance		
Diocesan	$42,753	$43,842
Parochial	$34,666	$33,120
Interparochial	$31,132	$34,275
Private: religious community-sponsored	$46,188	$44,164
Private: independent	$44,683	$45,650
Region		
New England	$44,158	$44,926
Mideast	$46,785	$46,000
Great Lakes	$40,580	$40,286
Plains	$40,261	$38,836
Southeast	$35,391	$34,754
West/Far West	$44,626	$43,253

The highest actual salary paid at an NAIS school, according to their reported data, was $53,039 (mean) and $51,961 (median).

Compensation: Administrators

Salaries for administrators who are not heads of school (associate or vice principals) vary somewhat according to governance types and region. In the one-third of schools that report a recent or long-standing president/principal model in place, administrative responsibilities of the associate principals could have shifted as a natural consequence of the president/principal leadership model, impacting compensation figures.

Exhibit 3.7 shows a national profile of administrative salaries excluding those earned by religious men and women whose compensation is not at lay equivalence.

Exhibit 3.7
National Profile of Administrative Salaries
(by Governance and Region)

	Mean	Median
National	$47,028	$46,390
Governance		
Diocesan	$46,800	$47,750
Parochial	$43,443	$42,183
Interparochial	$41,464	$41,000
Private: religious community-sponsored	$49,746	$48,700
Private: independent	$48,208	$50,000
Region		
New England	$45,534	$51,000
Mideast	$47,615	$47,500
Great Lakes	$47,196	$45,675
Plains	$46,299	$42,500
Southeast	$42,997	$42,703
West/Far West	$51,701	$53,175

The national average of a little over $47,000 has risen from $39,700 in 1994. Administrative salaries on the West Coast are somewhat higher than in other regions. In general, administrative salaries in private schools are among the highest; those in parochial schools are among the lowest, and those in arch/diocesan schools are at or near average levels. Associate head (vice-principal) salaries reported by NAIS reveal a mean of $76,517. The NASSP report indicates the mean salary for assistant principals in the range of $59,815 to $69,554, depending on the size of the school.

COMPENSATION: DEVELOPMENT DIRECTOR

A full-time salaried development director has become the norm in Catholic high schools. The average salary for this position in 1998-1999 was $40,600, up from $31,600 in 1994. Development director salaries vary widely, consistent with some wide variations in role description. While one director may be charged with conducting a moderate annual fund, another may be required to launch a major capital campaign. The NAIS mean salary for development directors is $61,471, about one-third greater than the salary paid in Catholic high schools.

Exhibit 3.8 shows comparative figures for development director salaries consistent with data relating to governance type and region.

Exhibit 3.8
Comparative Figures for Development Director Salaries
(by Governance and Region)

	Mean	Median
National	$40,588	$41,000
Governance		
Diocesan	$43,926	$35,500
Parochial	$30,630	$30,000
Interparochial	$31,237	$27,254
Private: religious community-sponsored	$45,858	$44,700
Private: independent	$47,855	$50,000
Region		
New England	$45,857	$48,750
Mideast	$39,936	$35,000
Great Lakes	$42,199	$43,950
Plains	$41,784	$36,000
Southeast	$35,910	$34,670
West/Far West	$42,829	$44,025

COMPENSATION: BUSINESS MANAGER

The average salary (excluding benefits) for the business manager in 1998-1999 was $36,268. In Exhibit 3.9, one can see some variation among private schools and diocesan schools and those sponsored by one or more parishes. The business manager's responsibilities, like the development director's, can differ in different institutions, and these distinctions may impact compensation figures.

The business manager's mean salary reported by NAIS was $69,626, considerably higher than the Catholic high school mean. Soft data indicate that in many cases the NAIS business manager assumes responsibilities beyond that of the typical Catholic school such as oversight for boarding school operations, extensive grounds maintenance, or investment portfolio management.

Exhibit 3.9
Average Salary (Excluding Benefits) for the Business Manager
(by Governance and Region)

	Mean	Median
National	$36,268	$35,345
Governance		
Diocesan	$33,038	$31,500
Parochial	$26,706	$26,390
Interparochial	$23,145	$22,000
Private: religious community-sponsored	$41,366	$40,052
Private: independent	$43,823	$49,000
Region		
New England	$31,617	$26,688
Mideast	$35,861	$33,900
Great Lakes	$38,979	$39,354
Plains	$34,461	$28,450
Southeast	$33,551	$31,000
West/Far West	$39,442	$40,000

COMPENSATION: BENEFITS

99% of all Catholic high schools provide standard health insurance to all employees. In over one-half of the schools, the employee is required to contribute to the premium. Roughly one-third of Catholic high schools provides fully-funded dental insurance. One-third provides it with a required employee contribution and the final one-third does not provide dental insurance. Vision insurance is the least provided benefit: only 15% offer it to their employees. Fully-funded disability is provided by slightly over one-half of Catholic high schools (55%) and life insurance is fully funded by 85% of the schools.

Only 6% of Catholic high schools report that they do not offer a retirement plan. 25% indicate a plan that requires employee contribution. 58% provide a retirement plan that is funded fully by the school with optional employee contributions.

Half of the schools use a retirement plan sponsored by the arch/diocese; 19% use TIAA-CREF; a small number use programs associated with sponsoring religious communities.

Almost all (95%) Catholic high schools offer their benefit plan to all employees; 5% offer it to full-time employees only.

Exhibit 3.10 shows the dollar value of the typical benefit package offered by the Catholic high school to employees.

Exhibit 3.10
Value of the Typical Benefit Package
(by Governance and Region)

	Mean	Median
National	$8,652	$6,000
Governance		
Diocesan	$9,406	$6,722
Parochial	$7,328	$5,262
Interparochial	$6,613	$5,242
Private: religious community-sponsored	$8,270	$6,096
Private: independent	$11,670	$7,648
Region		
New England	$8,122	$9,000
Mideast	$10,361	$7,500
Great Lakes	$7,806	$5,677
Plains	$11,466	$6,565
Southeast	$6,358	$5,752
West/Far West	$7,665	$6,192

CHAPTER 4

ADVANCEMENT IN THE CATHOLIC HIGH SCHOOL

Ninety percent of all Catholic secondary schools have established development offices with compensated staff. In 1994, this figure was 89%. Exhibits 4.1 and 4.2 show the distribution of titles for the position of the person in charge of the office. New titles such as "vice-president for advancement" are becoming more common among private Catholic high schools.

Exhibit 4.1
Distribution of Titles for the Head of Institutional Advancement
(by Governance and Region)

69%	Development director
4%	Vice president/principal for advancement
17%	**Other:**
	6% Director of institutional advancement
	3% President
	8% Miscellaneous
10%	Our school does not have a development office

Governance

	Diocesan	Parochial	Inter-parochial	Private: religious community-sponsored	Private: independent
Development director	80%	100%	84.2%	70.4%	61.1%
Vice president/ principal for advancement	1.7%	/	/	9.9%	11.1%
Other:	18.3%	/	15.8%	19.7%	27.8%
Other/Director of institutional advancement	10%	/	/	7%	11.1%
Other/President	3.3%	/	/	4.2%	/
Other/Misc.	5%	/	15.8%	8.5%	16.7%

Region

	New England	Mideast	Great Lakes	Plains	Southeast	West/Far West
Development director	81.8%	73.6%	70.3%	60%	85.7%	87.1%
Vice president/ principal for advancement	/	5.7%	8.1%	10%	/	3.2%
Other:	18.2%	20.7%	21.6%	30%	14.3%	9.7%
Other/Director of institutional advancement	/	13.2%	5.4%	15%	3.6%	/
Other/President	/	3.8%	2.7%	/	7.1%	/
Other/Misc.	18.2%	3.7%	13.5%	15%	3.6%	9.7%

The average Catholic high school opened a development office in 1987, although many schools launched offices well before that year. Exhibit 4.2 shows the years by type and region. The data indicate that development offices were likely to have been established earliest in the private independent Catholic high school. This longevity largely explains the higher percentage of alumni/ae participation in the annual fund in these schools.

Exhibit 4.2
Date of Opening a Development Office
(by Governance and Region)

	Mean	Median
National	1987	1989
Governance		
Diocesan	1988	1990
Parochial	1990	1992
Interparochial	1992	1993
Private: religious community-sponsored	1985	1986
Private: independent	1980	1980
Region		
New England	1985	1986
Mideast	1987	1989
Great Lakes	1986	1988
Plains	1985	1986
Southeast	1989	1990
West/Far West	1986	1987

THE ANNUAL FUND: ALUMNI/AE CONTRIBUTIONS

The alumni/ae contributions profiled in Exhibit 4.3 show significant growth since 1994. The average level of $76,195 has increased from $51,300 five years ago. Private schools consistently generate larger levels of funding from their alumni/ae. The parochial schools' level remains relatively modest, due in part to generally lower enrollments and to the reality of one or more sponsoring parishes, which may have comprehensive parish development programs.

Exhibit 4.3 shows the profile of alumni/ae contributions to the annual fund. The disparity between the mean ($76,195) and median ($30,000) is significant. Since half of the schools are above and half below the median, median amounts, unlike mean amounts, are not inflated by the substantial successes reported by a minority of schools.

Exhibit 4.3
Profile of Alumni/ae Contributions to the Annual Fund
(by Governance and Region)

	Mean	Median
National	$76,195	$30,000
Governance		
Diocesan	$50,371	$27,000
Parochial	$16,050	$0*
Interparochial	$18,182	$8,000
Private: religious community-sponsored	$118,569	$64,000
Private: independent	$130,368	$90,000
Region		
New England	$73,929	$14,500
Mideast	$121,946	$52,000
Great Lakes	$68,838	$33,000
Plains	$78,909	$47,500
Southeast	$42,357	$10,500
West/Far West	$45,364	$23,000

*More than 1/2 of the schools reported 0.

THE ANNUAL FUND: ALUMNI/AE PARTICIPATION

The percentage of alumni/ae participation in the annual fund across all domains of governance type and region is fairly impressive. While the national average rate of participation is 19%, a percentage achieved only after years of perseverance, one Catholic high school in the sample boasts a participation rate of 66%.

Here the closeness between the mean and the median suggests fairly even national performance distributions.

Exhibit 4.4
Percentage of Alumni/ae Participation in the Annual Fund
(by Governance and Region)

	Mean	Median
National	19%	15%
Governance		
Diocesan	12%	8%
Parochial	20%	15%
Interparochial	22%	15%
Private: religious community-sponsored	22%	20%
Private: independent	25%	26%
Region		
New England	16%	19%
Mideast	23%	15%
Great Lakes	17%	15%
Plains	32%	27%
Southeast	15%	14%
West/Far West	12%	11%

The Annual Fund: Parent Participation

The average contribution by parents to the annual fund has risen to $39,064 from $26,900 in 1994. Exhibit 4.5 displays some regional and governance variation, and again there is a marked gap between the mean and median. Low medians reflect large numbers of schools with little or no income from parents' annual gifts; higher means reflect the substantial success of a minority of schools.

Exhibit 4.5
Average Contribution by Parents to the Annual Fund
(by Region and Governance)

	Mean	Median
National	$39,064	$5,000
Governance		
Diocesan	$21,774	$3500
Parochial	$3,350	$0*
Interparochial	$11,227	$0*
Private: religious community-sponsored	$54,533	$10,500
Private: independent	$106,684	$110,000
Region		
New England	$55,786	$8500
Mideast	$31,168	$7500
Great Lakes	$31,892	$1000
Plains	$37,182	$0*
Southeast	$27,643	$0*
West/Far West	$68,818	$20,000

*More than 1/2 of the schools reported 0.

The responsibilities of the development director vary substantially based on school size, history, and mission. The comparison between 1994 and 1999 suggests that the position has become more clearly defined and, in some cases, additional staff have been secured. For example, some schools have added the position of annual fund director and realigned the development director's position with major gifts and capital campaign responsibilities.

Exhibit 4.6 outlines the major responsibilities reported by the schools completing the survey. The lower percentage for special events in 1999 indicates national growth in the position of development director. While events continue to provide an essential vehicle for community building and fundraising, they do not constitute the essence of Catholic high school development. These data suggest that role responsibilities in the Catholic secondary school are achieving greater clarity and focus.

Exhibit 4.6
The Responsibilities of the Development Director

	1999	1994
	yes	yes
Alumni/ae relations	67%	86%
Annual fund	78%	97%
Capital campaign	54%	78%
Long-range planning	40%	N/A
Major gifts	72%	N/A
Marketing/Recruitment	43%	34%
Planned giving	63%	N/A
Publications	66%	N/A
Special events	63%	85%

Annual fund goals vary considerably according to school governance type. The relatively high goals for private independent and private religious community-sponsored schools relate, in some part, to the earlier establishment of development offices in these schools.

Exhibit 4.7
National Profile of Annual Fund Goals (1998-1999)
(by Governance and Region)

	Mean	Median
National	$231,499	$150,000
Governance		
Diocesan	$152,046	$100,000
Parochial	$77,455	$50,000
Interparochial	$84,333	$72,500
Private: religious community-sponsored	$317,500	$237,500
Private: independent	$407,029	$370,000
Region		
New England	$273,030	$250,000
Mideast	$302,280	$117,500
Great Lakes	$236,333	$165,000
Plains	$194,305	$110,500
Southeast	$137,479	$97,500
West/Far West	$209,179	$167,500

Exhibit 4.7 shows marked distinctions in annual fund goals among schools. Private independent schools, followed by private religious community-sponsored schools have substantially higher annual fund goals than other schools. The most modest goals are those in parochial and interparochial schools. The parish(es) may have its own parochial development programs, an understandable reality that presents a challenge to the school(s) to develop its own constituency.

The obvious gap between the national mean and median merits analysis: the notably lower median suggests a high volume of goals in the lower ranges since half of the figures would lie below the median.

Exhibit 4.8 shows the complete national picture for contributions to the annual fund that come from sources other than alumni/ae or parents.

Exhibit 4.8
Annual Fund Contributions from Sources Other Than Alumni/ae or Parents
(by Governance and Region)

	Mean	Median
National	$57,513	$7,000
Governance		
Diocesan	$35,631	$5,000
Parochial	$6,600	$0*
Interparochial	$12,545	$0*
Private: religious community-sponsored	$101,097	$20,000
Private: independent	$68,263	$30,000
Region		
New England	$37,071	$11,500
Mideast	$64,042	$0*
Great Lakes	$80,611	$17,000
Plains	$44,043	$10,000
Southeast	$28,741	$0*
West/Far West	$60,545	$25,000

*More than 1/2 of the schools reported 0.

The category of "other" (pastor, past parent, grandparent, neighbor, corporation, foundation, faculty/staff member, and friend) contributions to the annual fund have remained amazingly consistent with 1994 data.

Exhibit 4.9 shows the (net) total generated in 1997-1998 from special events, excluding the annual fund.

Exhibit 4.9
Total Generated from Special Events, Excluding the Annual Fund (1997-1998)
(by Governance and Region)

	Mean	Median
National	$157,792	$84,500
Governance		
Diocesan	$149,103	$60,000
Parochial	$113,143	$34,000
Interparochial	$85,644	$65,000
Private: religious community-sponsored	$193,770	$100,000
Private: independent	$168,359	$148,982
Region		
New England	$54,125	$35,000
Mideast	$191,045	$68,000
Great Lakes	$210,589	$101,000
Plains	$174,099	$150,000
Southeast	$74,750	$62,500
West/Far West	$149,832	$92,650

Once again, the disparity between the national mean and median suggests a high volume of relatively low figures and some relatively high ones. One-half of the figures fall below the median point of $84,500 and one-half fall above that level, in contrast to the higher figure of $157,792 that represents the national average of revenues from special events.

Special events revenues have grown considerably. The 1994 report indicated $91,400 annual contribution from special events to the budget; the current figure, $157,792, represents a 73% increase in five years. In previous years, diocesan schools were more successful in generating revenue through special events. In the last five years, the average diocesan school's percentage has grown from $107,700 to $149,103, a 38% increase. During the same period, parochial and private school averages have more than doubled. This growth points to schools' success in using special events as donor cultivation and donor recognition tools as well as for revenue generation. Special events partner with solicitation-based annual funds; they highlight the essential aspect of community-building in the mission of the Catholic high school.

While the national mean reflects to a fair degree the net revenue produced by special events in the typical Catholic high school, the data reveal some notable achievements well beyond the norm: one school raised $2.5 million from special events.

The capital campaign has become a reliable means for Catholic high schools to generate substantial revenue for building construction, renovation, or program enhancement, for technology acquisition and infrastructure, and for launching or strengthening the endowment. About 35% of Catholic high schools were involved in a capital campaign in 1998-1999. This statistic serves as a dramatic sign of institutional health.

Many capital campaigns contain targeted endowment components. The national profile of Catholic high schools' endowments shows that endowments may be growing in importance. The gap between the national mean and the median indicates the high volume of modest endowments contrasted with some selected extraordinary ones. The data reveal that one school's endowment was valued at $46 million.

Larger endowments are found typically in private Catholic schools. This growth may be attributed to the particular model of governance in these schools, a model that generally includes a governing board with a broad range of responsibilities. The board's infrastructure is conducive to a close relationship between the head of school and the board and this partnership can create a favorable atmosphere for the raising of high-impact gifts, often from the board members themselves.

The disparity between means and medians is again significant. Means are inflated by substantial contributions from a relatively small number of very successful schools; medians provide a more accurate reflection of the typical Catholic high school's endowment.

Exhibit 4.10 shows the national endowment profile of the average Catholic high school.

Exhibit 4.10
National Endowment Profile
(by Governance and Region)

	Mean	Median
National	$1,890,614	$650,000
Governance		
Diocesan	$1,026,974	$450,000
Parochial	$265,917	$180,000
Interparochial	$1,291,177	$600,000
Private: religious community-sponsored	$2,760,034	$1,250,000
Private: independent	$2,967,960	$1,350,000
Region		
New England	$1,246,300	$500,000
Mideast	$2,317,641	$300,000
Great Lakes	$2,072,625	$1,500,000
Plains	$2,437,017	$1,000,000
Southeast	$936,496	$411,500
West/Far West	$1,593,977	$788,000

CHAPTER 5

LEADERSHIP AND GOVERNANCE IN THE CATHOLIC HIGH SCHOOL

Titles hold meaning when they offer realistic descriptions of the titleholders' service and contribution to the fulfillment of the school's mission. Some Catholic high schools have adopted the president/ principal model as a response to the expanded responsibilities necessarily assumed by the school's head. Like the role of a university president, the head of school's sphere of involvement includes increasing responsibilities related to the generation of resources. Consequently, the traditional position of principal has expanded and, like some stocks, it has split.

The data reveal that 46% of the heads of Catholic high schools hold titles other than "principal." While 46% indicate a title other than principal, only 29% of the schools in the sample use the title of "president." Yet, when asked, "Does your school have a president/principal (or similar) leadership model?" 46% responded affirmatively. These data suggest that while about one-third of the schools employ a model using the title "president," an additional 10% employ "something similar." Slightly fewer than one-half of the Catholic high schools in the country have adopted a leadership model distinct from the traditional one with the principal as head of school.

Exhibit 5.1
Titles for Heads of School
(by Governance and Region)

57%	Principal
29%	President
8%	Head
6%	Other (President-Principal, Superintendent, Administrator, Miscellaneous)

Governance

	Diocesan	Parochial	Inter-parochial	Private: religious community-sponsored	Private: independent
Principal	67.2%	95.8%	65%	40%	30%
President	23.4%	4.2%	20%	42.9%	35%
Head	3.1%	/	/	10%	35%
Other	6.3%	/	15%	7.1%	/

Region						
	New England	**Mideast**	**Great Lakes**	**Plains**	**Southeast**	**West/Far West**
Principal	61.5%	53.6%	56.8%	43.5%	68%	60%
President	15.4%	33.9%	37.8%	39.1%	16%	20%
Head	23.1%	8.9%	2.7%	8.7%	3.4%	11.4%
Other	/	3.6%	2.7%	8.6%	13.8%	8.6%

NEW LEADERSHIP MODELS

The Secondary Schools Department first reported the emerging leadership model of president/ principal in *Dollars and Sense: Catholic High Schools and Their Finances,* 1992 (M. Guerra). At that time, 80% of the respondents indicated that the title their head of school held was "principal." 20% held the title of "president." The subsequent report two years later provided the first trend data for analysis of the leadership model. In 1994, 24% of the respondents reported an institutional use of the term "president" and the current data reveal 29% using the title of "president"; yet, 46% use a title other than "principal." While the president/principal leadership design is the most commonly implemented non-traditional model, these data illustrate that it is not the only model serving Catholic high schools in a new way. Clearly, schools are being creative and imaginative in tailoring leadership structures that work.

Exhibit 5.2 shows the distribution of the leadership model where the head of school is someone with a title other than principal in Catholic high schools. The structure is used most frequently in Catholic private schools. Over 40% of the interparochial Catholic high schools have adopted the leadership model where the head of school is someone with a title other than principal, while only 28% of parochial high schools sponsored by only one parish have implemented it.

Exhibit 5.2
Schools That Report a Head of School with a Title Other Than Principal
(by Region and Governance)

	Head Other Than Principal	Head is Principal
National	46%	54%
Governance		
Diocesan	30%	70%
Parochial	28%	72%
Interparochial	41%	59%
Private: religious community-sponsored	63%	37%
Private: independent	69%	31%
Region		
New England	29%	71%
Mideast	50%	50%
Great Lakes	46%	54%
Plains	58%	42%
Southeast	40%	60%
West/Far West	44%	56%

For those schools that operate with a president, there are distinctions among school types in how the president is selected. In private independent schools, the board is the hiring body; in private religious community-sponsored schools, the hiring body could be the board, the religious community, or a combination of both.

Exhibit 5.3 shows the national and regional variations on the method of selecting a president.

Exhibit 5.3
Percent of Schools with Presidents Hired by Boards or Other Authorized Groups

37%	Board	
20%	Arch/diocese	
2%	Pastor	
27%	Religious community	
14%	**Other:**	
	3%	Other/Combo: Diocese and religious community
	6%	Other/Combo: Board and religious community
	5%	Other/Unspecified

Governance

Responsible for hiring president	Diocesan	Parochial	Inter-parochial	Private: religious community-sponsored	Private: independent
Board	16.7%	16.7%	25%	33.3%	100%
Arch/diocese	66.7%	16.7%	50%	2.2%	/
Pastor	/	/	/	/	/
Religious community	5.6%	33.3%	/	46.7%	/
Other:	11%	33.3%	25%	17.8%	/
Other/Combo: Diocese and religious community	5.6%	33.3%	/	6.7%	
Other/Combo: Board and religious community	5.4%	/	/	11.1%	/

GOVERNING BOARD CHARACTERISTICS

Governing boards are becoming increasingly important to Catholic high schools' stability and growth. The data point to an overwhelming majority of Catholic secondary schools with operational governing boards; four out of every five high schools in the sample report having a board in place.

Exhibit 5.4 shows the national profile of governing boards in the Catholic high school.

Exhibit 5.4
National Profile of Governing Boards in the Catholic High School
(by Governance and Region)

	Catholic High Schools with a Governing Board	Catholic High Schools without a Governing Board
National	81%	19%
Governance		
Diocesan	62%	38%
Parochial	58%	42%
Interparochial	100%	0%
Private: religious community-sponsored	95%	5%
Private: independent	100%	0%
Region		
New England	79%	21%
Mideast	74%	26%
Great Lakes	97%	3%
Plains	83%	17%
Southeast	77%	23%
West/Far West	79%	21%

The average board has sixteen members. The size of Catholic high schools' boards has not changed since the report, *Dollars and Sense: Catholic High Schools and Their Finances*, 1992 (M. Guerra). 81% of the members of boards are lay people, up from 74% in 1994. Private schools continue to have slightly fewer lay board members than diocesan or parochial/interparochial schools, possibly because religious communities have retained board positions in the schools they sponsor.

Responsibilities and expectations of board members have shifted somewhat since 1994, as illustrated in Exhibit 5.5.

Exhibit 5.5
Responsibilities and Expectations of Board Members

	1999	1994
Hires/renews/terminates school head's contract	54%	40%
Determines compensation of school head	50%	N/A
Evaluates school head	64%	40%
Approves operating budget	82%	82%

Exhibit 5.6 describes the level of influence boards have on Catholic high schools as perceived by their school heads. Survey respondents consider 95% of their boards to be either "very influential" or "somewhat influential," up from 75% in 1994. These data suggest the increasing importance of the board to the life of the school.

Exhibit 5.6
National Perceived Level of Board Influence
(by Governance and Region)

National

39%	Very influential
56%	Somewhat influential
5%	Not at all influential

Governance

	Diocesan	Parochial	Inter-parochial	Private: religious community-sponsored	Private: independent
Very influential	32.4%	21.4%	31.8%	40.9%	68.4%
Somewhat influential	64.9%	78.6%	54.5%	56.1%	26.3%
Not at all influential	2.7%	/	13.6%	3.0%	5.3%

Region

	New England	Mideast	Great Lakes	Plains	Southeast	West/Far West
Very influential	36.4%	35%	34.1%	60%	36.4%	40.7%
Somewhat influential	54.5%	60%	62.1%	40%	59.1%	55.6%
Not at all influential	9.1%	5%	3%	/	4.5%	3.7%

The data reveal that in schools where a president/principal model is operative, the president and principal both attend board meetings in 79% of the schools. This fact suggests a trend toward shared leadership in schools with a president. The practice of both administrators attending board meetings underscores the importance of both positions and the mutual respect required of the president, the principal, and the board.

Exhibit 5.7 shows the pattern of attendance at board meetings for presidents and principals.

Exhibit 5.7
National Attendance by Presidents and Principals at Board Meetings
(by Governance and Region)

National

9%	President only
79%	President and principal
6%	President/occasionally the principal
6%	Our school does not have a board (This percentage corresponds to only those schools that report having a president.)

Governance

	Diocesan	Parochial	Inter-parochial	Private: religious community-sponsored	Private: independent
President only	7.1%	/	/	8.7%	23.1%
President and principal	85.7%	100%	100%	82.7%	76.9%
President/ occasionally the principal	7.1%	/	/	8.7%	/
Our school does not have a board	/	/	/	/	/

Region

	New England	Mideast	Great Lakes	Plains	Southeast	West/Far West
President only	/	12.5%	5.6%	7.1%	10%	14.3%
President and principal	100%	75%	94.4%	92.9%	90%	71.4%
President/ occasionally the principal	/	12.5%	/	/	/	14.3%
Our school does not have a board	/	/	/	/	/	/

Chapter 6

Implications for the Future

> Much to cast down,
> much to build,
> much to restore;
> Let the work not delay,
> time and the arm
> not waste;
> Let the clay be dug
> from the pit.
> Let the saw
> cut the stone.
> Let the fire not be
> quenched in the forge.
>
> T.S. Eliot,
> "Choruses from 'The Rock'"

Mission and Money offers a challenge to the current and future leaders of Catholic secondary schools. True leadership in the Catholic high school requires the same skills demonstrated by great artists, who are likely to predict, even as they take pride in their highly celebrated portfolios, that their best work will be their next one. It means that completion of a project, like a major campaign, is really only a virtual concept, a brief slice of noted time in a never-ending continuum. The successful Catholic high school leader has learned to tolerate, to understand, and to manage seemingly disparate perspectives. The exceptional leader will ultimately appreciate what can be painful and exhausting about the creative process in strategic planning. Intense contrasts and tedium are both givens, to be understood as God's blessings, even when they feel like barriers. Leaders can neither rest for long on the laurels of success, nor marinade in the disappointments of setbacks. Confidence and humility must be simultaneously balanced. The leadership challenge for the future is to expand an ability to dwell in this domain of contrasts—so that completion and commencement are always partners.

The great European cathedrals bring daily joy to many who have access to their aesthetic wonder, sacred beauty, and religious utility. Yet, the warm candlelight of worship leaves its charcoal residue, and the scaffolding used for cleaning is also in continual, if not permanent, use. The maintenance crew, who cleans the pillars and ceilings of the cathedrals, takes pride in the emerging luster of the shimmering white marble, its chiseled surface restored to its earliest magnificence, knowing that the glowing candles' flames are already subtly depositing the crew's future workload. Catholic high school leaders, too, must move with willing anticipation to the next pillar in the circle of ever-finishing, never-ending work in fulfillment of the mission of Catholic secondary education.

Both builders and restorers rely on scaffolding. The modern scaffolding of vision, leadership, resources, and unshakable faith motivates Catholic high school leaders to know that nothing is beyond reach.

COMMENTARY ON MISSION AND MONEY

Mission and Money by Sister Mary E. Tracy is well done and provides a world of information and statistics on financial aid, tuition rates, compensation, the annual fund, and models of leadership and governance in Catholic secondary schools. The question is how is this data practical for school heads in the day-to-day running of the school and in particular in the financial management of the school.

While the financial aid chapter contains strong evidence of our commitment to help families of modest means send their children to our schools, it is important to note that all students in Catholic schools are receiving financial aid. All are subsidized because the tuition charged does not cover the full cost of education. For years, our schools have kept tuition low in order to make it possible for needy students to attend our schools. By doing this, we have subsidized those who could well afford to pay the full cost of education. The main reason this was possible in the earlier years was because of the role played by sisters, brothers, and priests, who worked for minimum salaries, salaries sufficient to cover their living expenses. This was a true endowment for Catholic schools. It is evident now that the building of an endowment is essential for all our schools. It is also evident that we need to ask those in our schools who can afford the full cost of education to donate the difference between the tuition charged and the actual cost of education.

It is clear from Sister Mary's data that the annual appeal and other fundraising activities are critical to the health and stability of the Catholic secondary school. With the decrease in religious teachers, the increase in lay faculty and administrators, and the efforts to increase salaries to a fair and just level, tuition will continue to fall short of meeting the needs of the operational budget. The dilemma that heads of schools face is simply this: tuition can only be increased so much before we price ourselves out of the market. Annual giving and other fundraising activities such as an auction can generate only so much money and cannot continue to increase each year. What is the solution? The solution is to begin to build an endowment for each and every school one step at a time, a permanent fund whose principal will not be touched and only a percentage of the earnings will be applied to the operation of the school each year. A recent educational bulletin suggested that educational leaders should plan now where the school could be in one hundred years. We all need that long-range vision now to make certain that our schools will be here and will have what they need one hundred years from now. Imagine what an endowment started now, as small as it may be, could be in one hundred years.

Chapter five on leadership and governance indicates the growth in lay leadership not only with administrators but also with governing boards. This chapter taken to heart should encourage heads of schools to actively recruit board members who can bring a variety of talents to their schools. Boards play a unique roll in helping the head of school achieve all the goals of the school and by providing leadership from many professional people who are committed to the school and to the education of the young men and women in the school. One key area board members can offer invaluable help in is in the area of development. Many of our alumni/ae are now successful business people and being board members gives them an opportunity to contribute in a meaningful way to the school that formed them in their teenage years.

In Sister Mary's last chapter, she calls us to fight the good fight and be brave. In plain language, she encourages us to continue the good work we are doing and to move ahead and provide our schools with excellent development staffs to meet the financial challenges that must be met to continue providing excellent education for our students. Those schools that are doing this should be encouraged to take the step to do more. Those schools doing little or nothing should take the step to begin now. Where do you want your school to be in one hundred years? What do you need to do now to begin to make that happen? Whatever it is, do it.

Rev. William Hayes, SJ, is Chancellor of Jesuit High School in Portland, OR.

COMMENTARY
ON MISSION AND MONEY

M*ission and Money* is a fine addition to the series of "big picture" research conducted by the NCEA. The data are quite provocative, and I believe this report will launch a thousand conversations among school leaders, board members, and diocesan officials.

My own conversations might begin by observing that the greater context for all of the report's financial data is the extraordinary growth in the U.S. economy over the past seven years. These were the best of times, and the Catholic secondary school ships were sailing in the fairest weather. What will happen when the economic weather turns foul – as it must, perhaps sooner than we think? Then the relationship between mission and money will really be tested, and many schools will unfortunately not survive.

Money fuels the mission; or as a sister who successfully managed Catholic hospitals told me, "No Margin, no Mission." Consider what happens to the school budget, which depends more than ever on tuition as the primary source of revenue (roughly 80% - up from 75% in 1994), when the low and modest income families served by the school feel the effects of an economic downturn. This is an important consideration since only 20% of Catholic secondary school families are in the "upper-middle" or "upper" income categories.

What can be done to strengthen Catholic secondary schools and to help them navigate through difficult economic times? The evidence is in the report – and it is encouraging. More schools have good governing boards (the 19% that do not have effective governing boards will be the most likely to founder in tough weather). More schools have leaders who understand the business-side of the school. More schools are paying attention to their endowments, which are the safeguards of budgets during difficult times (and which are the means to attract large planned gifts from the $4-6 trillion in assets that will be available from estates over the next ten years).

Conversations about *Mission and Money* will cause anxiety in some circles. But hopefully they will conclude with "Carpe Diem."

Daniel McKinley is Executive Director of Partners Advancing Values in Education in Milwaukee, WI.

COMMENTARY
ON MISSION AND MONEY

Sr. Mary E. Tracy, SNJM, presents in this publication, *Mission and Money*, a tool for leaders of Catholic secondary schools to use as a guide in institutional planning and evaluation. Here is the first thorough presentation of what school leaders need to analyze as they seek to insure institutional vitality. Catholic school personnel should feel challenged to study the trends, highlights, and figures presented in this publication in order to gain the knowledge needed to engineer the fiscal stability of their institutions. No longer does one have to wonder about the status of a school's endowment or of its medical benefits package in comparison to other like schools. The answers are clearly presented in *Mission and Money*.

As I read the manuscript of *Mission and Money*, I came to believe the publication will be an invaluable asset for Catholic school leaders. I also sense that the need for the data in this publication will lead to the 2nd edition that will further break out the data.

Congratulations to Sr. Mary E. Tracy, the Executive Committee of the Secondary Schools Department, and the CHS 2000 Advisory Committee which inspired *Mission and Money*.

The mission of Catholic secondary education to continue to pass the faith to future generations will be enabled by this document as schools "flesh out meaningful levels of institutional wellness."

Sister Margaret Ryan, OP, is the President of Aquinas High School in Bronx, NY.

APPENDIX A

INTRODUCTION

The typical Catholic high school does not exist. It is merely a statistical model derived from the means of various pieces of data in the sample. The models of Catholic high schools that follow may be useful as a gauge to measure experiences and situations. When working with these models, one should be mindful that the figures presented are simply averages, not expressions of what schools should ideally have. Each school is unique, comprised of many variables that influence its operation. Some of these variables are elastic; others can harden into constraints, depending on the prevailing institutional climate or circumstances.

Model of a Typical Parochial Catholic High School

The Parochial/Interparochial Catholic High School (n=47)

Teacher Salary and Benefits	Mean
Beginning salary—scheduled (1998-1999)	$18,591
Highest salary—scheduled (1998-1999)	$32,348
Highest salary—actual (1998-1999)	$33,012
Median salary (1998-1999)	$24,674
Benefit package (1998-1999)	$6,993

Administrator Salary	
Head of School: All profiles (n=44)	$43,154
Head of School: Lay man or woman (n=32)	$47,690
Head of School: Religious brother or sister (n=8)	$28,231
Head of School: Diocesan or religious priest (n=4)	$36,710
Development Director	$30,914
Business Manager	$25,039
Other administrators	$42,517

Finances	
Total (operating) income (1997-1998)	$1,602,216
Income from tuition and fees (1997-1998)	$998,444
Average 9th grade tuition (1998-1999)	$2,553
Total amount of financial aid (1997-1998)	$73,175
Average grant, financial aid (1997-1998)	$920

Boards *(77% of parochial/interparochial Catholic high schools have governing boards)* (n=36)

Average number of members	12
Average number of lay members	10

Advancement	
Annual fund goal (1998-1999)	$80,674
Alumni/ae contribution (1997-1998)	$17,048
Parents' contribution (1997-1998)	$7,037
Others' contribution (1997-1998)	$9,383
Capital campaign (1998-1999)	26% are conducting a capital campaign
Fundraising from special events (1997-1998)	$100,271
Endowment	$745,826

The Diocesan Catholic High School (n=65)

Teacher Salary and Benefits	Mean
Beginning salary—scheduled (1998-1999)	$22,102
Highest salary—scheduled (1998-1999)	$40,588
Highest salary—actual (1998-1999)	$42,753
Median salary (1998-1999)	$31,045
Benefit package (1998-1999)	$9,406

Administrator Salary	
Head of School: All profiles (n=54)	$44,268
Head of School: Lay man or woman (n=26)	$63,478
Head of School: Religious brother or sister (n=17)	$27,459
Head of School: Diocesan or religious priest (n=11)	$24,846
Development Director	$36,926
Business Manager	$33,038
Other administrators	$46,800

Finances	
Total (operating) income (1997-1998)	$3,242,750
Income from tuition and fees (1997-1998)	$2,529,705
Average 9th grade tuition (1998-1999)	$3,815
Total amount of financial aid (1997-1998)	$224,591
Average grant, financial aid (1997-1998)	$1,008

Boards *(62% of diocesan Catholic high schools have governing boards)* (n=40)	
Average number of members	17
Average number of lay members	13

Advancement	
Annual fund goal (1998-1999)	$152,046
Alumni/ae contribution (1997-1998)	$50,371
Parents' contribution (1997-1998)	$21,774
Others' contribution (1997-1998)	$35,631
Capital campaign (1998-1999)	26% are conducting a capital campaign
Fundraising from special events (1997-1998)	$149,103
Endowment	$1,026,974

MODEL OF A TYPICAL PRIVATE CATHOLIC HIGH SCHOOL

The Private Catholic High School (n=93)

Teacher Salary and Benefits	Mean
Beginning salary—scheduled (1998-1999)	$21,998
Highest salary—scheduled (1998-1999)	$40,860
Highest salary—actual (1998-1999)	$45,864
Median salary (1998-1999)	$32,292
Benefit package (1998-1999)	$9,001

Administrator Salary	
Head of School: All profiles (n=82)	$64,576
Head of School: Lay man or woman (n=25)	$75,241
Head of School: Religious brother or sister (n=38)	$58,379
Head of School: Diocesan or religious priest (n=19)	$62,939
Development Director	$46,287
Business Manager	$41,894
Other administrators	$49,415

Finances	
Total (operating) income (1997-1998)	$4,514,379
Income from tuition and fees (1997-1998)	$3,463,024
Average 9th grade tuition (1998-1999)	$5,510
Total amount of financial aid (1997-1998)	$337,832
Average grant, financial aid (1997-1998)	$2,041

Boards *(96% of private Catholic high schools have governing boards)* (n=89)	
Average number of members	17
Average number of lay members	13

Advancement	
Annual fund goal (1998-1999)	$336,754
Alumni/ae contribution (1997-1998)	$121,106
Parents' contribution (1997-1998)	$65,748
Others' contribution (1997-1998)	$94,036
Capital campaign (1998-1999)	39% are conducting a capital campaign
Fundraising from special events (1997-1998)	$188,305
Endowment	$2,804,749

Appendix B

National Summary of Mean Salaries of Heads of School

All Profiles	$53,248
Lay Head (n=83)	$60,934
Lay Man (n=64)	$59,798
Lay Woman (n=19)	$64,762
Sisters and Brothers (n=63)	$46,207
Sisters (n=39)	$47,332
Brothers (n=24)	$44,379
Priests (n=34)	$47,529
Diocesan (n=14)	$33,931
Religious Community (n=20)	$57,047

APPENDIX C

LIST OF PARTICIPATING SCHOOLS

NEW ENGLAND
Connecticut, Maine, Massachusetts, New Hampshire, Rhode Island, Vermont

Kolbe-Cathedral High School	Bridgeport, CT
St. Paul Catholic High School	Bristol, CT
Mercy High School	Middletown, CT
Canterbury School	New Milford, CT
St. Bernard High School	Uncasville, CT
Northwest Catholic High School	West Hartford, CT
North Cambridge Catholic High School	Cambridge, MA
Notre Dame Preparatory School	Fitchburg, MA
Presentation of Mary Academy	Methuen, MA
Newton Country Day School	Newton, MA
St. Clare High School	Roslindale, MA
St. Mary's High School	Westfield, MA
Cheverus High School	Portland, ME
Portsmouth Abbey School	Portsmouth, RI
Mount St. Charles Academy	Woonsocket, RI

MIDEAST
Delaware, District of Columbia, Maryland, New Jersey, New York, Pennsylvania

Georgetown Visitation Preparatory School	Washington, DC
St. Mary's School	Annapolis, MD
Mercy High School	Baltimore, MD
The Catholic High School of Baltimore	Baltimore, MD
The Seton Keough High School	Baltimore, MD
St. Maria Goretti High School	Hagerstown, MD
DeMatha Catholic High School	Hyattsville, MD
St. Mary's Ryken High School	Leonardtown, MD
Archbishop Spalding High School	Severn, MD
Bishop Francis Essex Catholic High School	East Orange, NJ
Hudson Catholic Regional High School	Jersey City, NJ
St. Mary's High School	Jersey City, NJ
Christian Brothers Academy	Lincroft, NJ

Immaculate Conception High School	Lodi, NJ
St. Benedict's Preparatory School	Newark, NJ
Roselle Catholic High School	Roselle, NJ
St. Mary's High School	Rutherford, NJ
Immaculata High School	Somerville, NJ
Oak Knoll School of the Holy Child	Summit, NJ
Lacordaire Academy High School	Upper Montclair, NJ
Immaculate Heart Academy	Washington Township, NJ
Cardinal Hayes High School	Bronx, NY
St. Catharine Academy	Bronx, NY
St. Helena Commercial High School	Bronx, NY
Fontbonne Hall Academy	Brooklyn, NY
Our Lady of Perpetual Help High School	Brooklyn, NY
St. Joseph High School	Brooklyn, NY
Holy Angels Academy	Buffalo, NY
St. Joseph's Collegiate Institute	Buffalo, NY
Holy Cross High School	Flushing, NY
The Mary Louis Academy	Jamaica Estates, NY
Salesian High School	New Rochelle, NY
La Salle Academy	New York, NY
Regis High School	New York, NY
St. Agnes Boys High School	New York, NY
McQuaid Jesuit High School	Rochester, NY
Our Lady of Mercy High School	Rochester, NY
Cathedral Preparatory Seminary	Rye, NY
St. Anthony's High School	So. Huntington, NY
St. Peter's Boys High School	Staten Island, NY
Bishop Ludden Junior-Senior High School	Syracuse, NY
Catholic Central High School	Troy, NY
Central Catholic High School	Allentown, PA
St. Gabriel's Hall	Audubon, PA
Sacred Heart High School	Carbondale, PA
Conwell-Egan Catholic High School	Fairless Hills, PA
Bishop McDevitt High School	Harrisburg, PA
Villa Maria Academy	Malvern, PA
Venango Christian High School	Oil City, PA
Cardinal Dougherty High School	Philadelphia, PA
Father Judge High School	Philadelphia, PA
Vincentian Academy-Duquesne University	Pittsburgh, PA
Cardinal O'Hara High School	Springfield, PA
Archbishop Wood High School	Warminster, PA
Bishop Neumann High School	Williamsport, PA
Bishop McDevitt High School	Wyncote, PA

Illinois, Indiana, Michigan, Ohio, Wisconsin

Marquette Catholic High School	Alton, IL
St. Viator High School	Arlington Heights, IL
Marmion Academy	Aurora, IL
Gordon Tech High School	Chicago, IL
Hales Franciscan High School	Chicago, IL
Mother McAuley Liberal Arts High School	Chicago, IL
Resurrection High School	Chicago, IL
St. Gregory High School	Chicago, IL
Benet Academy	Lisle, IL
Providence Catholic High School	New Lenox, IL
St. Bede Academy	Peru, IL
Quincy Notre Dame High School	Quincy, IL
Trinity High School	River Forest, IL
Mother Theodore Guerin High School	River Grove, IL
Sacred Heart-Griffin High School	Springfield, IL
Regina Dominican High School	Wilmette, IL
Mater Dei High School	Evansville, IN
Bishop Dwenger High School	Fort Wayne, IN
Roncalli High School	Indianapolis, IN
Cabrini High School	Allen Park, MI
University of Detroit Jesuit High School	Detroit, MI
Luke M. Powers Catholic High School	Flint, MI
Bishop Gallagher High School	Harper Woods, MI
Catholic Central High School	Redford Township, MI
Aquinas High School	Southgate, MI
Central Catholic High School	Canton, OH
St. Wendelin High School	Fostoria, OH
St. Joseph Central Catholic High School	Fremont, OH
St. Joseph Central Catholic High School	Ironton, OH
Newark Catholic High School	Newark, OH
St. Mary's Central Catholic High School	Sandusky, OH
Roger Bacon High School	St. Bernard, OH
St. John's Jesuit High School	Toledo, OH
Ursuline High School	Youngstown, OH
Xavier High School	Appleton, WI
Notre Dame de la Baie Academy	Green Bay, WI
Aquinas School	La Crosse, WI
Messmer High School	Milwaukee, WI
St. Joan Antida High School	Milwaukee, WI

PLAINS

Iowa, Kansas, Minnesota, Missouri, Nebraska, North Dakota, South Dakota

Bishop Garrigan High School	Algona, IA
Kuemper Catholic High School	Carroll, IA
Beckman High School	Dyersville, IA
Spalding Catholic High School	Granville, IA
St. John High School	Beloit, KS
St. Teresa's Academy	Kansas City, KS
Pacelli High School	Austin, MN
St. Mary's Jr./Sr. High School	Sleepy Eye, MN
Benilde-St. Margaret's School	St. Louis Park, MN
St. Thomas Academy	St. Paul, MN
St. Agnes High School	St. Paul, MN
St. Thomas Aquinas Mercy High School	Florissant, MO
Helias Interparish High School	Jefferson City, MO
Vianney High School	Kirkwood, MO
De Smet Jesuit High School	St. Louis, MO
Nerinx Hall High School	St. Louis, MO
St. Mary's High School	St. Louis, MO
Villa Duchesne School	St. Louis, MO
Mount Michael Benedictine High School	Elkhorn, NE
St. Francis High School	Humphrey, NE
Kearney Catholic High School	Kearney, NE
Pius X Central High School	Lincoln, NE
Creighton Preparatory School	Omaha, NE
St. Mary's High School	Dell Rapids, SD

SOUTHEAST

Alabama, Arkansas, Florida, Georgia, Kentucky, Louisiana, Mississippi, North Carolina, South Carolina, Tennessee, Virginia, West Virginia

St. Bernard Preparatory School	Cullman, AL
St. Jude High School	Montgomery, AL
Trinity Junior High School	Fort Smith, AR
Chaminade-Madonna College Prep. School	Hollywood, FL
Bishop Kenny High School	Jacksonville, FL
Archbishop Curley-Notre Dame High School	Miami, FL
St. Brendan High School	Miami, FL
St. John Neumann Secondary School	Naples, FL
Academy of the Holy Names High School	Tampa, FL
St. Pius X High School	Atlanta, GA
Bethlehem High School	Bardstown, KY
Holy Cross District High School	Covington, KY

Sacred Heart Academy High	Lexington, KY
All Saints High School	London, KY
Presentation Academy	Louisville, KY
Newport Central Catholic High School	Newport, KY
Vermilion Catholic High School	Abbeville, LA
St. Joseph's Academy	Baton Rouge, LA
St. Paul's School	Covington, LA
Vandebilt Catholic High School	Houma, LA
Catholic High School	New Iberia, LA
Cabrini High School	New Orleans, LA
Holy Cross High School	New Orleans, LA
St. Mary's Dominican High School	New Orleans, LA
Catholic High School of Pointe Coupee	New Roads, LA
Our Lady Academy	Bay St. Louis, MS
Cathedral High School	Natchez, MS
St. Benedict at Auburndale School	Cordova, TN
Father Ryan High School	Nashville, TN
Catholic High School	Virginia Beach, VA
Notre Dame High School	Clarksburg, WV
Central Catholic High School	Wheeling, WV

West/Far West

Alaska, Arizona, California, Colorado, Hawaii, Idaho, Montana, Nevada, New Mexico, Oklahoma, Oregon, Texas, Utah, Washington, Wyoming

Bourgade Catholic High School	Phoenix, AZ
Salpointe High School	Tucson, AZ
Servite High School	Anaheim, CA
Mercy High School	Burlingame, CA
De La Salle High School	Concord, CA
Bishop Amat High School	La Puente, CA
Conaty Loretto High School	Los Angeles, CA
Marymount High School	Los Angeles, CA
Sacred Heart High School	Los Angeles, CA
Villanova Preparatory School	Ojai, CA
Mercy High School	Red Bluff, CA
Notre Dame High School	Salinas, CA
Academy of Our Lady of Peace	San Diego, CA
Mission College Preparatory School	San Luis Obispo, CA
Mary Star of the Sea High School	San Pedro, CA
Cardinal Newman High School	Santa Rosa, CA
Alverno High School	Sierra Madre, CA
St. Mary's High School	Colorado Springs, CO

St. Mary's Academy High School	Englewood, CO
Sacred Heart Academy High School	Honolulu, HI
St. Labre Catholic Indian High School	Ashland, MT
Bishop Kelley High School	Tulsa, OK
St. Mary's Academy	Portland, OR
Blanchet Junior High School	Salem, OR
Incarnate Word Academy High School	Corpus Christi, TX
Bishop Lynch High School	Dallas, TX
Cathedral High School	El Paso, TX
Nolan Catholic High School	Fort Worth, TX
St. Agnes Academy	Houston, TX
Incarnate Word High School	San Antonio, TX
St. Paul High School	Shiner, TX
St. Joseph High School	Ogden, UT
Forest Ridge School of the Sacred Heart	Bellevue, WA
O'Dea High School	Seattle, WA
Bellarmine Preparatory School	Tacoma, WA

APPENDIX D

Mission and Money: A CHS 2000 Report on Finance, Advancement, and Governance provides in-depth information for comparison and analysis. The data was gathered using a 155-question survey that was sent to 300 sample Catholic high schools in the United States. The annotated questionnaire provides the national response (as a percentage) and the number of schools that responded to each question.

By its conclusion, the *CHS 2000* research project aims to accurately describe the Catholic high school in the millennium in its many facets. At the conclusion of the project, scholars who are interested in conducting secondary analyses may request access to the group data by sending a description of their proposed projects to the *CHS 2000* project director. Consistent with its commit-ment to the participating schools, data that could be used to identify particular schools will not be released.

Legend

Number indicates the number of schools responding

Are men religious paid on the same salary schedule as lay teachers?

36 yes (20%)

55 no (30%)

92 does not apply (50%)

Percentage indicates the national response percentage

CHS 2000

CHS 2000 Advisory Committee

James Cibulka, PhD
Professor and Chair
College of Education
University of Maryland
at College Park

Rev. Andrew Greeley, PhD
Professor of Social Sciences
The University of Chicago

Jeanne Griffith, PhD
Director, Division of Science
Resources Studies
National Science Foundation

Bruno Manno, PhD
Senior Fellow
The Annie E. Casey Foundation

Dominica Rocchio, SC, EdD
Secretary for Catholic Education
& Superintendent of Schools
Archdiocese of Newark, NJ

NCEA Secondary Schools Department
Michael J. Guerra
Executive Director
& Project Director

Mary Frances Taymans, SND, EdD
Associate Executive Director

Mary E. Tracy, SNJM
Associate Executive Director

Eileen A. Emerson
Research Associate

November 2, 1998

Dear Colleague:

The enclosed survey, which is being sent to a randomly selected group of Catholic high schools in the United States and Puerto Rico, represents the first of four focused studies of the *CHS 2000* project. Each Catholic high school will be asked to complete only one survey for one of the special studies. Last year you completed the initial comprehensive questionnaire for *CHS 2000* and we thank you. The positive rate of return for the initial survey resulted in high levels of data reliability and validity. Your participation in this first study on finance, governance, and development is essential to the project's success. We will not ask you to complete any additional questionnaires related to *CHS 2000*.

We have tested this survey with four different schools; from that experience we have concluded that the survey completion will take about two hours of total staff time. Some sections, such as finance or development, may be best completed by staff members (business manager, development director) designated by you.

The *CHS 2000* project promises to be of enormous benefit to Catholic high schools engaged in strategic planning. *CHS 2000: A First Look* will be published during the current academic year. We urge you to examine carefully the analyses and trends included in this first report.

The elected executive committee of our Secondary Schools Department prioritized *CHS 2000*, the major research project on our agenda, as singular in importance and influence. Thank you for your prompt completion of this survey. A return envelope is enclosed; please return your survey to us by **December 15, 1998.**

Count on our professional and prayerful support as you lead your school with unlimited promise.

Sincerely,

Michael J. Guerra
Executive Director
Secondary Schools Department

Sr. Mary E. Tracy, SNJM
Associate Executive Director
Secondary Schools Department

FINANCE, ADVANCEMENT, GOVERNANCE

November 1998

A project of the
National Catholic Educational Association's
(NCEA)
Secondary Schools Department

1077 30th Street, NW, Suite 100
Washington, DC 20007-3852
Phone: 202/337-6232
Fax: 202/333-6706
Email: nceasec@ncea.org
Website: www.ncea.org

INTRODUCTION

This survey is being distributed to the president, principal, or other chief administrative officer of a representative sample of Catholic secondary schools in the United States. It is assumed that in most cases the head of school will complete the survey, but if necessary, that responsibility may be delegated. In any case, all questions should be answered from the point of view of the school head.

Instructions for completing this survey are printed in the guidelines on page15. Wherever an asterisk ** appears, an explanation or definition related to that question will be found in the instructional guidelines.

CONFIDENTIALITY STATEMENT

NCEA's Secondary Schools Department will not release **any** information on **individual schools** to any person or office without the expressed written permission of the administrative head of the school.

Your responses will be used only for the good of the Catholic educational enterprise in the United States. They will be combined with those of other Catholic secondary schools and reported as group data. In addition to presenting composite data for schools, the report will present comparisons of groups of schools by type, size, or region of the country.

SCHOOL IDENTIFICATION   **CORRECTIONS, IF NECESSARY**

_____

_____

_____

_____

_____

(If the label above needs correction, please enter the necessary corrections in the space to the right of the label.)

BACKGROUND

1. Name of school head: _____

2. Title that the school head holds: _____

    Principal: 113 (66%)
    President: 57 (34%)

3. Name and title of person who completed this survey: _____

    _____

4. Phone number of the person named in question #3 if different from the school number:

    (_____) _____
    (daytime)

FINANCE

5. Who is considered the chief financial officer of your school?

33	president (22%)
	vice president of finance
68	business manager (45%)
50	other: specify title: Principal (33%)

6. Does your school have a business manager?

156	yes (76%)
49	no (24%)

7. What is the salary of your business manager, excluding benefits?

$36,268 = Mean

8. What are the primary responsibilities of the business manager? (Check all that apply).

155	tuition collections and accounts receivable (76%)
153	payroll and benefit management (75%)
66	manage school's investments (32%)
74	plant/maintenance operations (36%)
59	bookstore operations (29%)
56	cafeteria operations (24%)
0	other

9. How does your school handle tuition collection? (Check all that apply).

117	tuition is collected monthly by the school. (57%)
52	tuition is collected monthly by a tuition management company. (25%)
58	tuition is billed and collected in full at the start of each term. (28%)
0	other

10. In 1997-1998, what percentage of tuition revenue was uncollected?

16	0% (8%)
82	0-1% (42%)
38	1-2% (19%)
27	2-3% (14%)
33	More than 3% (17%)

11. How does your school handle tuition delinquencies? (Check all that apply).

186	school works with families (91%)
62	school uses a collection agency (30%)
101	school limits student access to classes (49%)
151	school withholds transcripts (74%)
0	other

12. Is your school's business office automated?

137	completely (71%)
22	for payroll only (11%)
16	other (specify): Partially automated (8%)
18	no, our business office is not automated. (9%)

13. How often does your school conduct a complete financial audit by an external agency?

124	annually (62%)
45	occasionally, but not annually (22%)
32	we do not use an external auditing agency (16%)

If you have one or more diocesan priests or religious on your faculty, please answer questions #14 to #22; otherwise go to question #23.

14. Are diocesan priests paid on the same salary schedule as lay teachers?

22	yes (12%)
57	no (31%)
104	does not apply (57%)

15. Are women religious paid on the same salary schedule as lay teachers?

61 | yes (33%)

83 | no (45%)

41 | does not apply (22%)

16. Are men religious paid on the same salary schedule as lay teachers?

36 | yes (20%)

55 | no (30%)

92 | does not apply (50%)

17. Do all diocesan priests teaching full-time in your school receive the same compensation, regardless of education or experience?

28 | yes, stipend is the same for all diocesan priests (16%)

16 | no, there is variation based on experience & education (9%)

128 | does not apply (74%)

18. Do all women religious teaching full-time in your school receive the same compensation regardless of education or experience?

68 | yes (41%)

42 | no, there is variation based on experience & education (25%)

55 | does not apply (33%)

19. Do all men religious teaching full-time in your school receive the same compensation, regardless of education or experience?

43 | yes (25%)

28 | no, there is variation based on experience & education (16%)

99 | does not apply (58%)

20. What is the average annual compensation (total of salary, benefits, housing, transportation, and stipends) paid to **diocesan priests** who teach full-time in your school? (if question does not apply, write "DNA")

Mean = $23,252

21. What is the average compensation (total of salary, benefits, housing, transportation, and stipends) paid to **women religious** who teach full-time in your school? (if question does not apply, write "DNA")

Mean = $28,767

22. What is the average compensation (total of salary, benefits, housing, transportation, and stipends) paid to **men religious** who teach full-time in your school? (if question does not apply, write "DNA")

Mean = $31,764

23. In the 1998-1999 school year, what is the average dollar amount of the benefit package paid by the school (e.g., pension, social security [employer's contribution only], medical insurance, life insurance) for a full-time lay teacher?

Mean = $8,651

24. In your school, is merit a factor in establishing teachers' compensation?

21 | yes (10%)

182 | no (90%)

25. Does your school have an official salary schedule related to levels of education and years of experience by which lay teachers' salaries are determined?

189 | yes (93%)

15 | no (7%)

If your school has a salary schedule, please answer the next two questions; otherwise go to question #28. (Figures are for the 1998-1999 scale.)

26. What is the **scheduled** salary paid to a beginning lay teacher with no previous teaching experience with a B.A./B.S. (excluding benefits)?

Mean = $21,292

27. What is the highest **scheduled** salary paid for an experienced lay teacher with an M.A./M.S. (excluding benefits)?

Mean = $39,106

28. What is the highest salary **actually paid** to any lay teacher at your school in 1998-99?

Mean = $42,294

29. What is the **median**** of the salaries actually paid to full time lay teachers in your school (excluding benefits)?

Mean (of median) = $30,241

30. Are some or all teachers represented during contract negotiations by some negotiating group?

44 yes (22%)

158 no (If "no," please skip to question #33.) (78%)

31. What is the total **number** of full-time teachers in your school who are represented during contract negotiations by some negotiating group? (If none, write "0.")

Mean = 8

32. What is the **number** of your full-time teachers who are represented by each of the following groups? (If none for a group, write "0;" these numbers should add up to the answer given for question #31.)

Mean
- 13   Diocesan or school group affiliated with the National Association of Catholic School Teachers
- 0   Diocesan or school group affiliated with the American Federation of Teachers
- 0   Diocesan or school group affiliated with the National Education Association
- 14   Diocesan or school group unaffiliated with any national union
- 9   Other local group
- 71   Other national group

33. What is the **number** of full-time teachers who have been on the staff of your school for the following lengths of time? (Place a number in each space. If none, write "0.")

Mean = 5.1

4	Less than a year
5	1 to 2 years
6	3 to 5 years
7	6 to 10 years
5	11 to 15 years
4	16 to 20 years
5	21 to 30 years
2	31 to 40 years
16	41 + years

34. What is the **average** salary (excluding benefits) paid to full-time administrators (excluding the business manager and development personnel)? (In calculating the average, exclude religious administrators who receive stipends rather than equivalent lay salaries.)

Mean = $47,028

35. What is the salary (excluding benefits) paid to the head of school? (*Reminder: Your answers are confidential. No information on any school will be released without written permission from the head of school.*)

Mean = $53,247

36. If the head of school is president or someone with the title other than principal, what is the salary (excluding benefits) paid to the principal?

Mean = $18,106

37. What standard insurance benefits are included in your employees' compensation? (Check all that apply)

	school funds fully	school funds partially, employee contributes	not provided by the school
medical	79 (39%)	117 (57%)	6 (3%)
dental	64 (31%)	73 (36%)	52 (25%)
vision	29 (14%)	45 (22%)	94 (46%)
disability	110 (54%)	38 (19%)	41 (20%)
life insurance	129 (63%)	35 (17%)	29 (14%)

38. Does your school offer a retirement program?

116 (65%)   yes, a **defined contribution** plan, funded fully by the school, employee contribution optional.

36 (20%)   yes, a **defined contribution** plan, funded by the school and required employee contributions.

14 (8%)   yes, a **defined benefit** plan funded by the school with required employee contribution.

0   other

12 (7%)   the school does not currently offer any retirement plan.

39. If you answered "yes" to question #38, does the retirement program apply in the same way to all employees? If no, explain:

All: 151 (83%)

Full-time only: 20 (11%)

One or more years on staff: 10 (6%)

40. Which retirement program is used by your school?

37   TIAA-CREF (22%)

11   a program sponsored by the sponsoring religious community (7%)

98   a program sponsored by arch/diocese (58%)

23   other (specify):
401(K) or 403(B): 14 (8%)
Christian Bros. Retirement: 9 (5%)

41. What was the total **number** of students in your school in grades 9-12 in May, 1998?

Mean = 541

42. What **number** of your students in grades 9-12 received financial aid from your school in 1997-1998?

Mean = 112

43. Does your school consider any of the following criteria in awarding financial aid, in whole or part? (check **yes** or **no** for each criterion)

yes	no	
103 (53%)	92 (47%)	Academic record or promise
8 (8%)	88 (92%)	Athletic record or promise
196 (98%)	5 (2%)	Financial need
35 (18%)	162 (82%)	Racial or ethnic origin
6 (3%)	189 (97%)	Vocational intention
142 (72%)	56 (28%)	Faculty/Staff children
0	0	Other

44. Of the following criteria, which is given the **greatest** weight in awarding your school's financial aid funds? (check **one** only)

4   Academic record or promise (2%)

0   Athletic record or promise

192   Financial need (97%)

1   Racial or ethnic origin (1%)

0   Vocational intention

45. Do you use a standardized financial aid application?

34   yes, it is provided by the arch/diocese (30%)

6   yes, it is provided by a national organization (5%)

56   yes, it is developed by our school (50%)

0   other

16   no (14%)

46. What percentage of applicants for admission in 1998 requested financial aid?

Mean = 27%

47. At what level are you able to meet financial aid requests?

55 All students who need aid receive some aid. (28%)

88 Most (75-90%) students who express need receive aid. (45%)

31 Many (50-74%) students who need aid receive it. (16%)

12 Some (25-49%) receive it. (6%)

9 Financial aid is available for a small percentage (1-24%) of those who request assistance. (5%)

48. Financial aid is funded by: (Check all that apply.)

145 Operating scholarship budget (annual fund) (71%)

112 Restricted funds (55%)

93 General endowment funds (45%)

23 Other: Arch/diocese (11%)

49. Is a student work program part of the financial aid program at your school?

33 yes, for all financial aid recipients (16%)

56 yes, though it is optional (28%)

114 no (56%)

50. What was the **total** amount of financial aid, (including scholarships, tuition reductions, grants, work-study, and support from sponsoring parishes, dioceses, and religious orders) awarded in 1997-1998 by your school to students?

Mean = $245,950

51. What was the dollar value of the **average** financial aid allocation for one student?

Mean = $1,467

52. Give your best estimate on what **percent** of your students come from families with each of the following gross annual incomes? (Percents should add up to 100. If none in the category, write "0.")

	Percent
Low income (under $20,000)	12%
Modest income ($21,000-$40,000)	30%
Middle income ($41,000-$80,000)	36%
Upper-middle income ($81,0000-$120,000)	15%
Upper income (Over $121,000)	7%
Total	100%

53. Are the percentages you gave for question #52 estimates or accurate figures?

101 Figures are rough estimates (56%)

74 Figures are reasonable estimates (41%)

5 Figures are accurate (3%)

54. What percent of your students come from families who receive public assistance?

Mean = 6%

55. Does your school receive state or federal support for these services? (check all that apply)

57 reduced lunches (28%)

63 Title I services (31%)

105 textbooks and materials (51%)

81 transportation (40%)

70 faculty in-service programs (34%)

70 technology and telecommunications (34%)

55 mandated services (attendance, testing) (27%)

6 capital improvement (e.g. energy efficiencies, environmental requirements) (3%)

11 other (specify): Title VI (5%)

56. What is the **number** of students who applied (that is, completed the application process) for admission to your school's entry-level grade for the year 1998-1999?

Mean = 236

57. If you have grades lower than 9th grade, do you require a re-admission process for grade 9?

13   yes (7%)

44   no (23%)

136   does not apply (70%)

58. What is the **number** of students who were informed of acceptance to your entry-level grade in 1998-1999?

Mean = 191

59. What is the **number** of students, if any, who were put on a waiting list?

Mean = 16

60. Of the number given for question #59, how many were <u>not</u> accepted for admission?

Mean = 26

(Note: the numbers in questions #58, #59 and #60 should equal the number in question #56.)

61. Of the students accepted, what is the number of students who enrolled?

Mean = 155

62. How often do you consider each of the following in a student's application for admission to your entry-level grade? (For each, check **one**.)

	Always	Usually	Some-times	Rarely or Never
Ability to pay full tuition without aid	9 (5%)	28 (14%)	26 (13%)	134 (68%)
Completion of one or more standardized achievement or aptitude tests	121 (61%)	35 (18%)	13 (7%)	28 (14%)
Completion of written admissions test developed by your school	47 (24%)	15 (8%)	11 (6%)	119 (62%)
Personal interview with parent or guardian	66 (33%)	29 (15%)	72 (36%)	32 (16%)
Recommendation of elementary school principal	92 (46%)	46 (23%)	46 (23%)	15 (8%)
Recommendation of student's pastor	17 (9%)	24 (12%)	77 (39%)	80 (40%)
Strong academic record	101 (52%)	49 (25%)	19 (10%)	25 (13%)
Successful completion of previous year of school	179 (90%)	17 (9%)	4 (2%)	0

63. Of the students who enroll at the entry-level grade of your school, about what percentage would you estimate remain in your school and graduate?

2   100% (1%)

56   95%-99% (28%)

63   90%-94% (32%)

47   80%-89% (24%)

25   70%-79% (13%)

6   Less than 70% (3%)

64. In what year was your school established?

Earliest: 1799; Latest: 1996
(87 schools between 1946 and 1970)

65. In what year was the oldest building that currently houses your school built?

Earliest: 1799; Latest: 1998
(107 between 1959 and 1971)

66. What is your best estimate of the current market value of the school buildings and grounds?

Mean = $9,574,765

67. Who holds title to the land and buildings occupied by the school?

61	Religious community (31%)
89	Arch/diocese (46%)
14	Parish (7%)
30	School corporation (15%)
0	Other

68. If your school were at maximum enrollment, how many students could your facility serve?

Mean = 695

REMINDER: Your answers are confidential. No information on your school will be released without permission from the head of school.

Please indicate the school's **1997-1998** income and operating expenses, using the categories shown. **Reminder**: Definitions and exact guidelines for all items bearing an asterisk (*) will be found in the instructional guidelines on page 17.

Please make an entry on every line. This will considerably increase the accuracy of our final report.

SOURCES OF INCOME
(round to the nearest thousand dollars —
e.g. $12, 675 should be recorded as $13,000)

69. Tuition and fees

Mean = $2,619

70. Contributed services**

Mean = $65,000

71. Subsidy or grant from religious community

Mean = $16,000

72. Subsidy or grant from parish

Mean = $75,000

73. Subsidy or grant from diocese

Mean = $48,000

74. Other subsidy or grant

$0

75. Alumni/ae contribution to annual fund**

Mean = $76,000

76. Parents' contribution to annual fund

Mean = $39,000

77. Other contributions to the 1997-1998 annual fund

$0

78. Fundraising from special events

Mean = $111,000

79. Net income from auxiliary services (excess of income over expenses)

Mean = $52,000

80. Income from federal government sources

Mean = $12,000

81. Income from state government sources

Mean = $19,000

82. Income from endowment transferred to operating budget

Mean = $59,000

83. All other income

Mean = $175,000

84. Total operating income (should equal sum of question #69 to question #83)

Mean = $3,366,000

OPERATING EXPENSES
(round to the nearest thousand dollars —
e.g. $243,490 should be recorded as $243,000)

85. Salaries-lay professional staff, including development office

Mean = $1,346,000

86. Salaries-religious professional faculty/staff (actual cash paid)

Mean = $158,000

87. Contributed services**

Mean = $61,000

88. Other salaries (e.g., general office, maintenance, but not auxiliary services)

$237,000

89. All fringe benefits paid by the school (FICA, health insurance, retirement, unemployment, etc.)

Mean = $322,000

90. Net expenses for all auxiliary services**

Mean = $65,000

91. Maintenance costs

Mean = $208,000

92. All other operating costs

Mean = $606,000

93. Total operating expenses (should equal sum of question #85 to question #92)

Mean = $3,003,000

94. What is the 1998-1999 tuition? This is the "base tuition" for a student who is the only student from a given family, and before allowances and discounts. What was the 1997-1998 tuition? Please fill in one answer for each blank. If your school does not have one or more of these grades, write "DNA".

	1998-99 tuition	1997-98 tuition
Grade 7	Mean = $4,091	$3,970
Grade 8	Mean = $4,019	$3,641
Grade 9	Mean = $4,289	$4,055
Grade 10	Mean = $4,297	$4,053
Grade 11	Mean = $4,433	$4,054
Grade 12	Mean = $4,304	$4,038

95. Is there a reduction in tuition when more than one child in a family registers in the school?

131 yes (66%)

68 no (34%)

96. Is there a reduction in tuition when a student is the child of a teacher or administrator?

173 yes (87%)

25 no (13%)

ADVANCEMENT

97. What title does the primary advancement/development staff person hold?

140 development director (77%)

9 vice president/principal for advancement (5%)

13 other: Director of Institutional Advancement (7%)

21 our school does not have a development office (11%)

98. Which of the following staff positions do you fund in your school? (Please indicate all that apply.)

163 development director (or similar) (80%)

32 annual fund director (16%)

88 administrative assistant for development (43%)

54 public relations director (or similar) (26%)

79 alumni/ae director (39%)

90 admissions (recruitment) director (44%)

8 other: Special Events Director (4%)

99. In what year did your school first establish a paid development director position?

Mean = 1987; Earliest: 1956; Latest: 1998

100. How many years has your development director been in his/her position at your school?

75 two years or fewer (43%)

33 three to five (19%)

29 five to eight (17%)

20 eight to twelve (12%)

16 twelve or more (9%)

101. What is the highest level of education of your development director?

17 some college, no degree (10%)

89 bachelor's degree (51%)

67 master's degree (38%)

2 doctoral degree (1%)

102. Which of the following responsibilities are assumed by your development director? (indicate all that apply)

[132] alumni/ae relations (64%)

[153] annual fund (75%)

[107] capital campaign (52%)

[78] long-range planning (38%)

[141] major gifts (69%)

[85] marketing (42%)

[120] planned giving (59%)

[131] publications (64%)

[129] special events (63%)

[0] other

103. If your school has a full time director of development, what is that person's salary (excluding benefits)? *(Reminder: Your answers are confidential. No information about any school will be released without written permission from the head of school.)*

Mean = $40,589

104. Does the development director attend board meetings?

[99] yes (57%)

[40] no (23%)

[34] occasionally (20%)

105. Does your school have a development committee?

[134] yes (72%)

[52] no (28%)

106. If you answered "yes" to question #105, is the development committee a standing board committee?

[112] yes (84%)

[22] no (16%)

107. Which board committees, if any, does the development director staff?

[118] development (74%)

[11] board operations/nominating (7%)

[31] marketing (19%)

[0] other

108. What is your current (1998-1999) annual fund goal?

Mean = $231,498

109. What percentage of your alumni/ae contributed to your 1997-1998 annual fund?

19%

110. Is your school currently conducting a capital campaign?

[68] yes (34%)

[133] no (66%)

111. How many capital campaigns has your school completed in the past two decades?

Mean = 1.08

112. What is the (net) total that your school raised in 1997-1998 from special events, excluding annual fund? (round off to nearest thousand)

Mean = $157,792

113. What is the size of your school's endowment?

Mean = $1,890,614

114. What development software does your office use?

[58] Blackbaud's (Raiser's Edge) (53%)

[7] Donor Perfect (6%)

[9] JSI (Paradigm) (8%)

[9] Fundmaster (8%)

[27] Our development office is not equipped with software. (25%)

[0] other

115. Does your advancement/development office have internet access?

| 143 | yes (76%) |
| 44 | no (24%) |

116. Does your school use a Harris Directory** (or similar) for alumni/ae?

| 133 | yes (72%) |
| 51 | no (28%) |

117. Does your school have an established alumni/ae association**?

| 140 | yes (73%) |
| 51 | no (27%) |

118. Does your development office promote bequests and other planned gifts?

| 133 | yes (72%) |
| 52 | no (28%) |

119. Estimate the number and dollar amounts of bequests and other planned gifts received over the past five years.

#: Mean = 23
$: Mean = $874,443

120. Have you hired a development consultant in the last five years?

| 107 | yes (55%) |
| 86 | no (45%) |

121. If you answered "yes" to question #120, on what project(s) did the development consultant advise?

79	capital campaign (41%)
41	office operations and role clarity (21%)
27	development audit (14%)
27	planned giving (14%)
17	board operations/retreat (9%)
0	other

122. If you answered "yes" to question #120, with which resources did you work?

15	NCEA (24%)
11	Catholic School Management (18%)
4	Independent School Management (6%)
32	other: 24 Private consulants (39%); 8 Community counsel services (13%)

123. How does the development director relate to the parent association?

39	no formal relationship (23%)
73	occasionally, through special events (42%)
29	attends most meetings, but not key staff person (17%)
22	primary staff liaison to parent association (13%)
10	the school does not have a parent association (6%)

124. How often does the development director meet with the head of school?

81	more than once a week (46%)
61	once a week (35%)
26	twice a month (15%)
7	rarely (4%)

125. To what professional organizations related to advancement/development does your school belong?

58	CASE (Council for Advancement and Support of Education) (20%)
31	NAIS (National Association of Independent Schools) (11%)
151	NCEA (52%)
49	NSFRE (National Society of Fund Raising Executives) (17%)
0	other

126. What local and/or national conferences does your development director generally attend?

35	CASE (25%)
14	NAIS (10%)
64	NCEA Advancement strand during annual convention (46%)
27	other: 11 Arch/diocesan (8%); 15 NSFRE (11%)

GOVERNANCE

127. Does your school have a governing board**?

   | 164 | yes (81%) |
   | 38 | no (19%) |

If you have a governing board, please answer questions #128 to #145; otherwise go to question #147.

128. What is the composition of your board in terms of members of the laity and members of religious communities or diocesan priests?

   Mean = 13   # of lay board members

   Mean = 2.6   # of religious board members

   Mean = 1   # of diocesan priests

   Mean = 16   **total**

129. In approximately what year was your board formed?

   Mean = 1982; Median = 1944

130. In your opinion, what is the degree of influence the school board has on your school's operations? *(School head's opinion requested here.)*

62	very influential (39%)
89	somewhat influential (56%)
7	not at all influential (4%)

131. Check all that apply to your board's responsibilities:

89	hires/renews-terminates contract of school head (54%)
82	determines compensation of school head (50%)
105	evaluates school head (64%)
134	approves operating budget (82%)
10	does not apply (6%)

132. If your answer to question #131 is "does not apply," who fulfills the responsibilities outlined in question #131?

11	sponsoring religious community (33%)
15	arch/diocese (45%)
7	pastor (21%)
0	other

133. Which of the following situations best describes your school (check one)?

34	Board is independent. (22%)
59	Board is accountable to corporate Board of Members of a religious community. (38%)
36	Board is accountable to arch/diocese. (23%)
21	Board is accountable to pastor(s). (14%)
4	Other: Accountable to head of school (3%)

134. What standing board committees does your school have? (check all that apply)

114	executive committee (70%)
82	long-range planning (50%)
146	finance (89%)
111	building/grounds (68%)
69	board operations/nominating/trusteeship (42%)
37	marketing (23%)
106	development (65%)
66	education (40%)
23	personnel (14%)
32	investment (20%)
0	other

135. How often does your board meet?

71	monthly (49%)
44	quarterly (30%)
30	other (specify): 5 or 6 times annually (21%)

136. Does your board hold a regular self-evaluation?

| 60 | yes (37%) |

| 104 | no (63%) |

137. What percentage of your board members gives to the annual fund?

| 52 | 100% (32%) |

| 44 | 80-99% (28%) |

| 22 | 50-79% (14%) |

| 21 | less than 50% (13%) |

| 21 | we do not have an annual fund. (13%) |

138. Does your board hold a retreat on a regular basis? (If your answer is yes, please answer questions #139 and #140. If your answer is no, proceed to question #141).

| 49 | yes (30%) |

| 115 | no (70%) |

139. For what purpose(s) does the board use the retreat?

| 10 | for planning purposes only (19%) |

| 4 | for spiritual growth only (8%) |

| 39 | for both planning and spiritual growth (74%) |

| 0 | other |

140. Does your board use the expertise of an external facilitator for the retreat?

| 27 | yes (47%) |

| 12 | no (21%) |

| 18 | occasionally (32%) |

141. Has one or more of your board members attended in the last seven years a conference on trusteeship?

| 62 | yes (40%) |

| 92 | no (60%) |

142. If you answered "yes" to question #141, who sponsored the conference?

| 7 | CASE (13%) |

| 7 | NAIS (13%) |

| 11 | NCEA (20%) |

| 30 | other (specify): 10 Religious community (18%); 16 Arch/diocese (29%); 4 JSEA (7%) |

143. Does your school provide directors and officers liability insurance?

| 93 | yes (58%) |

| 67 | no (42%) |

144. If your school is sponsored by a religious community, does the community leadership approve board members before they join the board?

| 55 | yes (53%) |

| 49 | no (47%) |

145. If your school is sponsored by an arch/diocese, does the bishop or his delegate approve board members before they join the board?

| 28 | yes (36%) |

| 49 | no (64%) |

146. If your school is sponsored by a parish or parishes, does the pastor(s) approve board members before they join the board?

| 20 | yes (43%) |

| 27 | no (57%) |

147. Does your school have a president/principal (or similar) leadership model**?

| 94 | yes (47%) |

| 108 | no *(If "no," survey is complete)* (53%) |

148. If you answered "yes" to question #147, who hires the president?

[33] board (43%)

[18] arch/diocese (23%)

[2] pastor and board (3%)

[24] religious community (31%)

[0] other

149. If you answered "yes" to question #147, which of the following administrators attend the board meetings?

[8] president only (9%)

[72] president and principal (79%)

[5] president/occasionally the principal (5%)

[6] our school does not have a board (7%)

150. Does the president hire the principal?

[50] yes (56%)

[40] no (44%)

151. If you answered "no" to question #150, who hires the principal?

[17] board (49%)

[11] arch/diocese (31%)

[1] pastor (3%)

[6] religious community (17%)

[0] other

152. If you have a president/principal model, who signs the contracts of your school personnel?

[23] president (27%)

[26] principal (31%)

[12] president signs some, principal signs some (14%)

[23] president and principal sign all (27%)

153. In your president/principal model, who signs the students' diplomas?

[8] president (9%)

[20] principal (22%)

[61] president and principal (69%)

154. In your president/principal model, who staffs the parent council?

[10] president (13%)

[27] principal (34%)

[18] shared by president and principal (23%)

[3] staffed by other than president or principal (4%)

[21] our school does not have a parent council (27%)

155. In your president/principal model, who is considered to be the leader of institutional advancement/development?

[66] president (79%)

[12] principal (14%)

[6] other (7%)

We welcome any additional comments you care to make:

_____

_____

_____

_____

_____

MAILING INSTRUCTIONS

Thank you for your participation in this important work. Please return this survey by **December 15, 1998** in the enclosed return envelope addressed to

Michael J. Guerra, Project Director
CHS2000
NCEA Secondary Schools Department
1077 30th Street, NW, Suite 100
Washington, DC 20007-3852.

We are most grateful for your cooperation in providing this important service for Catholic secondary education.

NCEA's Secondary Schools Department will not release **any** information on **individual schools** to any person or office without the expressed written permission of the administrative head of the school.

INSTRUCTIONAL GUIDELINES

#29. *Median* refers to the halfway point in a list of items, a point where half of the items would be above the point and half below the point (e.g. the median of 9 would be 5; the median of 8 would be 4.5). Median is not to be confused with mean (average) or mode (most common).

#70. *Contributed Services* is defined as the difference between the actual cash salaries paid to religious (including personal expenses such as housing or transportation paid on their behalf) and lay equivalent salaries (If a religious were a lay person, what would the lay compensation be?). Contributed services should be counted as income and expense.

Contributed Services should be computed as follows:

Valuation of religious personnel at lay
compensation equivalence (salary and benefits)
$_____

Less actual cash compensation (salary and benefits)
$_____

Less actual cash to cover personal expenses
(such as transportation and housing)
$_____

(Net) Value of Contributed Services
$_____

#75. *Annual fund* refers to a revenue generating program that is solicitation-based; it excludes special events, capital campaign or funds transferred from endowment interest.

#90. *Auxiliary Services:* Income and expenses from auxiliary services should be netted, a net gain providing an additional source of revenue, while a net loss is an additional expense. Otherwise, gross revenue would be misleading, and total expenses would distort educational expenses, per pupil costs, etc. The usual auxiliary services are cafeterias, bookstores, bussing, facility rentals, dormitories, and summer camps.

#115. *Harris Directory* (or similar) refers to an alumni/ae directory of addresses and phone numbers compiled by a for-profit company; alumni/ae are invited to purchase a directory.

#117. An *established alumni/ae association* would have some or all of these characteristics: association officers (president, secretary, treasurer), regular meetings, annual events (Memorial Mass, luncheon, golf tournament, or similar).

#127. *Governing board* is meant to include all boards: those with full policy direction and those in an advisory capacity.

#147. The *president/principal leadership model* is in place at a number of Catholic high schools. Traditional and emerging responsibilities are divided between the two roles. The president generally assumes an external role of mission articulation and resource development; the principal assumes the role of primary instructional leader.